[sizzle!]

modern australian barbecue food

modern australian barbecue food

sizzle!

by Allan Campion and Michele Curtis

photography by Adrian Lander

conran
OCTOPUS

PROPS

Minimax

585 Malvern Road Toorak 9826 0022

Gempo Living 1800 443 366

Graham and Annie for the world's best
barbecue apron

Hayley Inverarity for her red esky

RECIPE INSPIRATION FROM

The Cook's Companion,
Stephanie Alexander, Viking 1996

Spice, Christine Manfield, Viking 1999

Gourmet Barbecue Cookery,
Charmaine Solomon, Fontana 1987

The Classic Barbecue and Grill Cookbook,
Marlena Spieler, Dorling Kindersley 1996

www.weber.com

www.bbq.about.com

AND

Sue Sloan for green bean salad

Will Studd for pancetta and pecorino
vine leaves

Lynda Grace for chilli crabs

Laurence de Zoete for caramelised onions

AND FINALLY THANKS TO

Jonathan Gianfreda for the cevapcici
recipe and his excellent lamb

Peter Bouchier for the steak signs

Elizabeth Vella for assisting with the
food preparation

Max and Sophie Allen for their input

Penelope Steuart for her continuous
support and enthusiasm

Published in 2001 by Conran Octopus Limited
2–4 Heron Quays, London E14 4JP, UK

Text and recipes copyright
© Allan Campion and Michele Curtis
Wine text copyright © Max Allen
Photographs copyright © Adrian Lander
Design copyright © Ian Scott

First published by Purple Egg in 2000

Designers: Ian Scott and Chris Raybould
Editor: Elizabeth Vella
Anglicisation: Jo Smith
Senior Editor (UK): Katey Day
Production Controller: Alex Wiltshire

British Library Cataloguing-in-Publication Data
A catalogue record for this book is
available from the British Library.
ISBN 1 84091 197 2

Printed in China by Toppan

To all our friends who entered our garden and sizzled with us.

A special thank you to Teresa Campion who gave us a barbecue as a house-warming present; we couldn't have done it without you.

[contents]

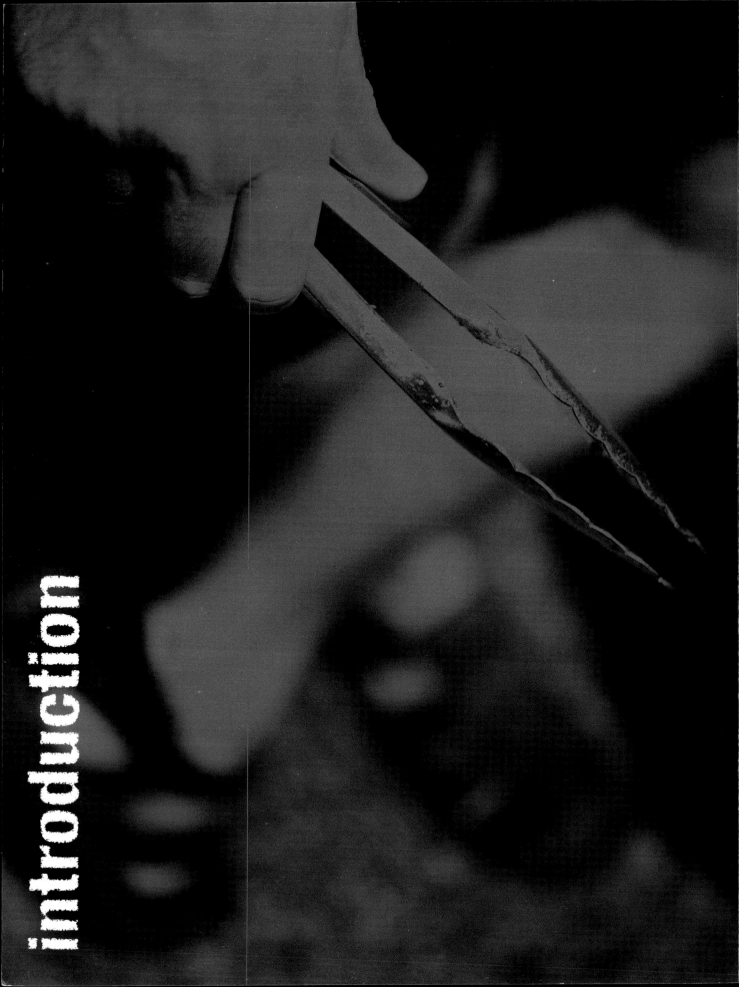

introduction

[introduction]

Are you ready to sizzle?

Personally speaking, we Sizzle! whenever the weather permits – and even when it doesn't. Everything from rosemary and garlic-studded lamb on a spit, perfectly barbecued sausages, whole smoky salmon or juicy char-grilled steaks. In fact, barbecuing is something we enjoy so much we decided to write a book about it.

Sizzle! has been a pleasure to write (and cook for) from beginning to end. We've driven our neighbours crazy with delicious aromas wafting over the fence and had more than one pet visiting for tasty titbits.

The best thing about barbecuing is that anyone can do it, and everyone loves the thrill of mastering the barbecue, tongs in hand. Cooking outdoors makes food look good, smell good and taste great. There's also a great atmosphere created by the combination of a hot smoky grill, platters of food, cool salads, chilled drinks and the relaxed open-air feeling.

So gather together family and friends and get ready to Sizzle!

Allan Campion and Michele Curtis

choosing and using a barbecue

Chances are you already have a barbecue. After cooking from Sizzle! for just one summer you'll probably have worn it out, so bear this chapter in mind.

Available space is a big consideration and this will dictate whether you need a trolley, kettle or open fire barbecue. Advice is also given on the different fuels available, such as charcoal, lava rocks and even timber. In addition, there's help with choosing essential accessories to make your barbecuing experience a pleasurable one.

A barbecue that is used and kept properly will not only result in correctly cooked food, but healthy food too. It is important to clean your barbecue to make it last, after all, you do clean the kitchen after you've cooked dinner – don't you? Greasy barbecues are not only a health hazard, but also a fire hazard. Look after your barbecue and it will return the favour with many summers worth of happy meals.

Gas barbecues

Gas barbecues are convenient and quick to use.

They consist of a timber or metal frame, sometimes with both a hotplate and a grill for cooking.

Stainless, solid steel or cast aluminium constructions will last longer in the great outdoors.

They usually have small benches on each side that are perfect for utensils, oil and plates.

Trolley barbecues also come as 'outdoor kitchens', complete with rotisseries and wok burners.

In Sizzle! we see barbecuing as cooking directly on a barbecue grill or plate.

If you want to learn how to cook with a wok, seek out a book that deals directly with that method.

Gas barbecues are linked to a gas bottle that will require frequent filling.

a good trolley barbecue should have:

- a pull-out drip tray that is easy to access
- a sturdy frame and strong wheels
- an automatic ignition
- a small table on each side for utensils and ingredients
- at least two burners under each grill or hotplate to allow for different cooking temperatures.

LIGHTING UP

Turn gas to high under the section you want to cook on and allow to heat for 15 minutes.

Reduce heat to desired temperature before cooking.

In Sizzle! we recommend cooking on a medium-high heat unless otherwise stated.

SIZZLING TIME

Simply brush a thin layer of olive oil onto barbecue plate or grill before adding food.

Olive oil on a piece of kitchen paper will do the trick.

This stops food sticking to the barbecue plate or grill.

If you have trouble with food sticking, simply leave for 1 minute and try again.

To cook large pieces of meat, or to speed up cooking time, cover food with a lid.

The lid can be as simple as a piece of kitchen foil, a metal bowl, or better still, a wok lid.

A lid is particularly useful when cooking thick steaks, or meat on the bone.

Flare-ups cause blackening of the food and unpleasant tastes.

Flare-ups usually occur as fat (or excess marinade) drips down.

Drain food well and remove excess fat before cooking.

CLEANING UP

Scour grill with a wire brush straight after taking food off.

Then raise gas to high and leave for 3–4 minutes.

This will burn off any remaining fat and food scraps.

While the barbecue plate is hot, remove food scraps with a new paint scraper.

Use kitchen paper to wipe over all barbecue surfaces.

When cold, brush plate and grill with cooking oil and cover barbecue until required.

Ensure gas bottle is turned off.

From time to time the entire barbecue will need to be taken apart and each part washed in hot soapy water, dried with newspaper and re-assembled.

This is a good time to change the absorbent material in the drip tray and run a wire brush over the gas jets.

LAVA ROCKS
CERAMIC ROCKS
HEAT DIFFUSER

Lava rocks (or volcanic rocks), ceramic rocks and solid metal heat diffusers are placed between the gas jets and grill to act as a heat conductor.

These stop gas flames reaching the food, store heat and radiate it upwards to create a hot surface over which to cook.

Over time lava rocks will soak up fat and cease to conduct heat.

Ceramic rocks (which require a grid to sit on) prevent flare-ups, last even longer than lava rocks, and provide a more even heat.

These take longer to heat up.

Ceramic rocks and the grid are worthwhile investments if you use your barbecue extensively.

A heat diffuser is a metal grid designed to go between the gas jets and the grill.

While all rocks impart some flavour to the food, the flavour imparted by heat diffusers is negligible.

HOW MUCH GAS IS LEFT?

You can't tell by shaking the bottle.

Remove bottle from barbecue and stand it on a flat surface.

Pour boiling water over one side of the bottle and allow to cool.

Run your hand over where the water was poured.

The cold area indicates how much gas is in the bottle.

Easy!

FAT SOAKER

Fat soaker lives in the drip tray beneath the gas jets.

Fat soaker does exactly what it says.

Do not use sand as it rusts the tray.

Cat litter is not recommended as it contains a deodorant that will taint your food and may catch fire.

Change fat soaker regularly, as fat-soaked fat soaker will ignite.

Kettle barbecues

Kettle barbecues now come in a host of different styles, the traditional charcoal and the gas-fired, both in endless shapes and sizes.

Gas-fired kettle barbecues do away with the inconvenience of lighting them.

You can roast or grill in a kettle barbecue and this imparts wonderful flavours.

You can also use smoking chips to add more flavour to your food. Mesquite wood chips are one of the most popular. Soak in water for one hour before use.

The compact, circular shape of the kettle barbecue makes it ideal for smaller spaces, such as balconies.

LIGHTING UP

The key to cooking well in a kettle barbecue is lighting it properly.

This is best done in a spot out of the wind and requires your attention to ensure a proper cooking temperature is reached.

Place 6 briquettes or pieces of charcoal in a row on each side of the barbecue lower rack. Top these with 3 firelighters, 6 more briquettes or pieces of charcoal, 2 more firelighters and a final 6 briquettes or charcoal pieces.

Metal containers to hold the charcoal and lighters are available.

Light firelighters and keep watch to ensure they flame well (add a little more charcoal if needed).

You may need to fan the fire to keep it going at a good speed.

The charcoal will have to burn to a white-ash stage before any cooking takes place.

Arrange the charcoal on the sides of the barbecue for kettle (indirect) cooking or push them to the centre for regular (direct) cooking.

When this stage is reached, place the lid on the barbecue and open top and bottom vents.

The barbecue will now remain hot for up to an hour before you start cooking.

SIZZLING TIME

Place a foil tray beneath the charcoal to catch drips.

Add flavoured wood chips to create a smoky flavour to the food if desired.

Insert the upper cooking rack.

Place food to be cooked on upper rack in the centre of the kettle barbecue.

Either leave lid off, cooking over the embers as you would with any barbecue, turning food as necessary (direct heat); or cover with lid to create an oven effect (indirect heat), and do not move the food during cooking.

CLEANING UP

Kettle barbecues need to cool completely before cleaning.

Sweep all ash into bottom tray and discard.

Remove both wire racks and rub gently with a wire brush.

Wash inside of barbecue and then dry with newspaper.

Do the same for the outside of the barbecue.

Put barbecue back together and cover until required again.

Cold ash is excellent on the garden.

Open-fire barbecues

Dedicated barbecuers consider this their best source of heat.

It could be a rack balanced on a pile of bricks over a fire, a hibachi or a charcoal-lit barbecue.

You have to wait until the fire dies down to red embers before you can cook on it.

The fire can be made with wood, charcoal or briquettes.

Charcoal can be a hard wood based such as mesquite, or manufactured such as briquettes.

Wood is much more unpredictable and difficult to control.

Never use treated wood.

Different types of wood produce different flavours.

Never cook food over full red flames; this produces charred meat with raw centres.

Use smoking wood chips to add other flavours as desired.

LIGHTING UP

To prepare a wood fire, place twists of newspaper and kindling on the bottom.

Light and allow to catch fire.

Gradually add twigs, small sticks and finally larger sticks as fire takes hold.

Lastly, add logs and allow to burn down to red embers – this will take $1\frac{1}{2}$–$2\frac{1}{2}$ hours.

Experience will show the amount of fuel needed.

Once you have red embers, there is little you can do to adjust the heat they produce.

To prepare a charcoal fire, either use newspaper and kindling as described, or use firelighters beneath charcoal, as described in kettle barbecues.

Charcoal is ready to cook over once it is covered with white ash.

SIZZLING TIME

Brush barbecue plate or grill with oil before placing food on.

If the fire is really hot, brush food with oil.

Watch carefully when using a fire (before, during and after cooking) to make sure it doesn't get out of control, or children get too close.

Enjoy the wonderful flavours that an open fire produces.

Try wrapping potatoes, onions and other vegetables in kitchen foil and cooking them in the red embers.

This source of heat is ideal for toasting marshmallows.

CLEANING UP

Allow fire to cool completely.

Scrape out ash and cold embers and discard.

Cold ash is excellent on the garden.

Clean grill or plate with a wire brush.

Brush grill and plate with oil.

Accessories

UTENSILS

A wire brush with strong bristles is essential for cleaning.

Use long-handled tongs to prevent burnt fingers.

A new triangular paint scraper, 5 cm (2 in) wide, is good for turning food and scraping food scraps away.

Use long matches for lighting to prevent burnt fingers.

Aprons are good for preventing splashes on clothing.

VINE CLIPPINGS

Vine clippings add a beautiful flavour to food.

Red wine vines are the preferred type, cabernet sauvignon in particular.

Vine clippings are available from barbecue or charcoal suppliers.

To use, begin a fire with wood or charcoal and prepare to glowing coals.

Add a handful of vine clippings to the coals; allow flames to die down then place food on the grill to cook as normal.

Vine clippings are ideal for game, beef or lamb.

SKEWERS

Skewers are indispensable when barbecuing.

They can hold tricky ingredients, such as squid, flat for cooking, and make small ingredients easy to turn and move about on the barbecue.

Skewers also provide something to hold onto while eating.

Wooden skewers must be soaked in cold water for at least an hour before use to ensure they do not burn.

Metal skewers are easier still, as they never burn or splinter. Simply thread ingredients on.

Use rosemary branches, sugar cane, or lemongrass stalks for more flavour.

Get to know your barbecue's hot and cold spots, then you can move food around accordingly.

Rub or brush barbecue lightly with oil just before cooking any ingredients.

[barbecue rules]

Use meats that don't have too much fat on them, as fat will cause flames to flare up and singe the food (forget 'BBQ' lamb chops).

Food will take longer to cook on a windy day as wind reduces the heat.

A cold beer will keep your fingers cool during cooking.

A sure-fire way to ruin a good piece of meat is to pour beer or wine over it during cooking.

Forget that your father has done it all his life. In effect, you are cooling the barbecue and wasting precious alcohol.

Never barbecue in bare feet.

COOKING TIPS

Place meat on barbecue, cook as recommended, then rotate 180 degrees. Turn over, rotate once more.

Do not flip-flop the meat around.

Always cook longer on the first side.

You should only have to turn it over once.

Never cut into meat to see if it is cooked as the juices escape. See page 74 – How well cooked is your steak?

Allow large cuts of meat to rest for 5 minutes before serving.

Take the recipes in Sizzle! and make them your own.

The recipes in Sizzle! will produce food cooked to perfection. Recipes indicate whether this is medium-rare or cooked through. Simply adjust cooking times to your preference.

Cooking times will vary from barbecue to barbecue.

In Sizzle! we recommend cooking on a medium-high heat unless otherwise stated.

HEALTH TIPS

Never place raw meat in full sun.

Bring food from the kitchen just before cooking.

Never put cooked meat back onto a platter that has had raw meat on.

Ensure meat is cooked correctly, especially pork and chicken, which must be cooked through.

Do not 'char' your food.

GLOSSARY

For any ingredients you are unsure of, check the glossary on pages 162–163.

Ingredients marked with an * are explained in the glossary.

key to sizzling methods

 Barbecue Grill

 Barbecue Hotplate

 Kettle Barbecue

marinades and spice blends

One of the simplest ways to add extra zing to your food is to marinate it before cooking. But beware, over-marinating will render your meat soggy and the flavours too strong. Make sure you drain the food well before adding to the barbecue or you will not Sizzle! Use remaining marinade for basting during cooking. As a general rule, do not marinate for longer than 4 hours, the exception being very large pieces of meat and octopus.

Adding spice can be as simple as olive oil and freshly ground black pepper, or some wonderfully scented blend that contains up to 16 different ingredients. No marinating is necessary, just rub on and get cooking.

2¹/₂ tbsp tomato ketchup

1 tbsp Worcestershire sauce

1 tbsp white vinegar

4 tsp brown sugar

2 tsp Dijon mustard

1 tsp chilli powder

Dash of Tabasco

spicy barbecue marinade

Whisk ingredients together.

Good on pork, beef or chicken.

4 tbsp olive oil

4 tbsp wine of your choice

2 shallots, finely diced

2 garlic cloves, crushed

3 tsp chopped fresh herbs

Salt and freshly ground black pepper

basic wine marinade

Mix all ingredients together.

Use white wine for white meats,

red wine for dark meats.

oriental marinade

1 tbsp black beans*, soaked and drained

100 ml (3¹/₂ fl oz) soy sauce

1 tbsp Thai fish sauce

2 tsp chilli paste

1 tsp sesame oil

2 tsp grated ginger

Mash black beans with a fork.

Add remaining ingredients.

Good on chicken or pork.

spicy mexican marinade

Mix all ingredients together.

Good on chicken or beef ribs.

1 garlic clove, crushed

¹/₂ tsp salt

¹/₂ tsp chilli powder

1 tsp paprika

¹/₂ tsp ground coriander

¹/₂ tsp ground cumin

1 tsp yellow mustard seeds, crushed

¹/₂ tsp freshly ground black pepper

1 tbsp olive oil

lemon marinade

Place onions in a food processor and purée to a fine paste.

Place a clean tea towel over a bowl and pour onion purée into it.

Squeeze all juice into the bowl then add lemon juice and salt.

Marinate chicken fillets for a maximum of 2 hours.

Pat fillets dry before using.

2 onions, chopped

4 tbsp lemon juice

1 tsp salt

soy and garlic marinade

Mix all ingredients together.

Good on all meats and fish.

1 tbsp rice vinegar

2 tbsp soy sauce

1 garlic clove, crushed

Pinch of five-spice powder

1 tsp caster sugar

A few drops of Tabasco

caribbean fish marinade

Mix all ingredients together.

Marinate fish for 30 minutes.

3 tbsp lime juice

1 tsp ground allspice

3 spring onions, thinly sliced

1 small red chilli, finely diced

$\frac{1}{2}$ tsp salt

2 tbsp olive oil

4¹/₂ tsp paprika

3 tsp onion powder

creole blend

3 tsp garlic powder

Mix together well.

1¹/₂ tsp thyme leaves

Good on fish.

1¹/₂ tsp ground oregano

1 tsp cayenne pepper

1 tsp white pepper

1 tsp freshly ground black pepper

1 tsp ground coriander

1 tsp ground cumin

simple moroccan blend

1 tsp paprika

Mix to form a smooth paste.

¹/₃ tsp salt

Good on fish and lamb.

1 tbsp lemon juice

2 tbsp olive oil

salt and pepper spice

3 tsp Sichuan pepper*

Place pepper and salt in a dry pan and cook over a medium heat.

¹/₂ tsp salt

Stir until the salt turns golden, approx 3 minutes.

¹/₂ tsp five-spice powder

Crush in a mortar and pestle until very fine.

Sieve to remove husks and stir five-spice through.

Good on oily fish, quail, prawns and chicken.

nibbles

Everyone needs some nibbly things to keep them going while the barbecue warms up. Dips and breads are just one of the options. Quick bread or Indian bread are ideal with babaganoush or tzaziki (page 142). Bruschetta with various toppings can be prepared in advance, while there is a whole host of suggestions in the 'other ideas' box, including lime and chilli chicken wings, beef satay sticks and barbecued oysters.

Babaganoush is a Middle Eastern aubergine dip.

6 Lebanese (long thin) aubergines

Brush aubergines with oil.

Olive oil

Place on oiled barbecue grill.

1 garlic clove, crushed

Cook for 30 minutes, turning often, until soft and charred.

1½ tbsp lemon juice

Allow to cool. **babaganoush**

1½ tbsp tahini

Peel away charred skin and place flesh in a bowl.

90 g (3 oz) natural yoghurt

Mash until smooth.

Pinch each of ground allspice,

Add remaining ingredients, adjust seasoning to taste.

white pepper and salt

≡ Sizzling time 30 minutes

Lay vine leaves out flat.

Place 1 slice of pancetta in the centre of each.

12 vine leaves*

Cover with pecorino. **pecorino and pancetta**

12 thin slices pancetta*

Fold vine leaves over to enclose ingredients. **vine leaf parcels**

200 g (7 oz) mature pecorino cheese, sliced thinly

Place on oiled barbecue plate and cook for 1½ minutes on each side.

■ Sizzling time 3 minutes

Makes 12

This quick bread recipe is simple to make and produces bread not unlike pitta.

Mix flour, oil and salt together.

Pour boiling water on top and stir to bring the dough together.

150 g (5 oz) self-raising flour

Knead until it forms a soft dough. **quick bread**

2 tbsp olive oil

Divide into four and roll each piece out to a thin circle.

Pinch of salt

Dust each with flour to prevent sticking.

125 ml (4 fl oz) boiling water

Brush each bread lightly with oil.

Cook on oiled barbecue hotplate for 2 minutes or until just brown.

Turn over and cook on remaining side for further 2 minutes.

■ Sizzling time 4 minutes

Makes 4

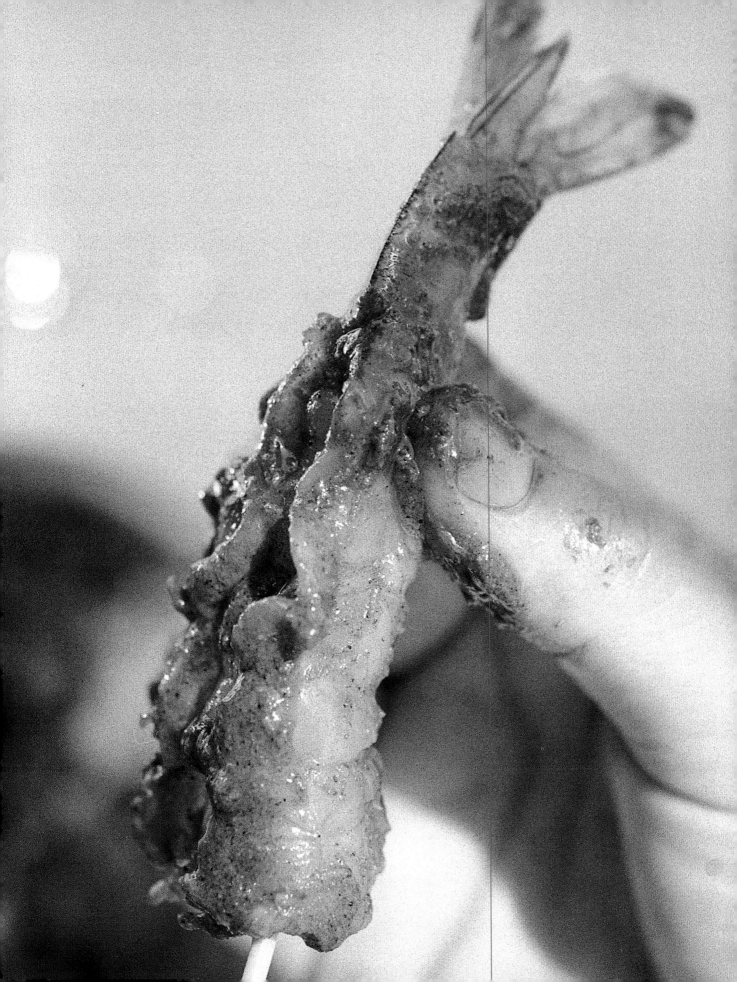

2½ tbsp warm water

1 tsp caster sugar

2 tsp (1 sachet) dry yeast

3 tsp caster sugar

1 egg

1 tsp salt

125 ml (4 fl oz) natural yoghurt

150 ml (5 fl oz) milk

150 ml (5 fl oz) water

50 g (1³/₄ oz) melted butter

700 g (1½ lb) plain flour

Extra flour as needed

Olive oil for cooking

Mix water, 1 tsp sugar and yeast in a bowl and leave until it froths a little.

Stir in all the next 7 ingredients, then gradually stir in the flour.

The dough should be fairly sticky at this stage.

Sprinkle extra flour on the work surface, place dough on top.

Knead dough for 6–8 minutes, adding extra flour to get rid of any stickiness.

The dough should have a silky feel when ready.

Place in an oiled bowl and allow to prove in a warm place

until doubled in size, about 1–2 hours.   **indian bread**

Knead dough for 1 minute, then divide into 16 equal portions.

Using a rolling pin or your fingers, make each bread 20 cm (8 in) across.

Place a tight layer of clingfilm on a dinner plate and lay bread on it.

Cover with more clingfilm and repeat until all breads are ready.

Cook bread on oiled barbecue hotplate a few at a time.

Cook for 2 minutes each side.

■ Sizzling time 4 minutes

Makes 16

Brush with garlic butter (page 62) for garlic Indian bread.

The Indian bread can have spices such as ground cardamom, cumin and coriander added to the dough during making to create different flavours. Add 3 teaspoons per batch.

Tuna teriyaki skewers

Caribbean garfish

1 French stick

Olive oil for cooking

4 garlic cloves, peeled and halved

Cut bread into 1 cm (½ in) slices.

bruschetta Brush each slice with a little oil.

Cook on oiled barbecue grill until golden, turning regularly.

When cooked rub each slice with garlic.

Top with one of the suggested toppings below.

Sizzling time 2–3 minutes

TOPPINGS:

Tomato and fresh herb salsa (page 140)

Soft goat's cheese and tapenade

Roasted aubergine and pesto

Smoked salmon, sour cream and horseradish

Other ideas

Tunisian sardines (page 34)

Thai fish cakes (page 35)

Tuna teriyaki skewers (page 36)

Chermoula prawns (page 47)

Sizzlin' garlic prawns (page 48)

Green chilli and kaffir lime calamari skewers (page 50)

Oysters two ways (page 52)

Lime and chilli chicken wings (page 58)

Mexican spicy drumlets (page 59)

Pandan chicken parcels (page 62)

Kashmiri quail (page 67)

Beef satay kebabs (page 77)

Satay pork sugar cane sticks (page 97)

fish

To some, it may be unusual to cook fish on the barbecue, while others have long since realised the full flavour potential of cooking fish over hot coals. Simple fish fillets basted with herb butter are hard to resist. Small whole fish such as red mullet or sardines are delightful, while whole salmon or snapper will bring a whopper of a sensation to the dinner table.

Firm white fish fillets are the best for the barbecue, as they will not fall to pieces. Try monkfish, haddock, sea bass, cod, huss, bream or other local varieties. Oily fish are ideal too, but should be cooked medium-rare to prevent them drying out – try tuna, trout, swordfish and shark. Find yourself a good fishmonger, one who will remove all the fiddly bones from the centre of fillets such as salmon, and who will clean and scale whole fish to save you the hassle. Wrapping fish in kitchen foil or banana leaves produces a moister fish as it steams while cooking, but it will take slightly longer to cook.

Fish goes well with fresh herbs, garlic and lemon. Asian flavours such as ginger, Thai fish sauce, lemongrass and chillies work well too. Oily fish cope better with strong flavours and spice.

Fish sizzling times

2 minutes Sardine fillets

6 minutes Fish fillets 2cm (3/4 in) thick

6 minutes Fish steaks

5–7 minutes Oily fish fillets, medium-rare

15 minutes Small whole fish, unwrapped

20 minutes Small whole fish, wrapped

1 hour Large whole fish

50 g (1³/₄ oz) soft butter

2 tsp chopped fresh herbs

Grated zest of 1 lemon

Freshly ground black pepper

4 x 200 g (7 oz) firm white fish fillets

Combine butter, herbs, lemon zest and pepper together.

Place butter in a heatproof bowl on the side on the barbecue.

simple barbecued fish
Place fish on barbecue hotplate.

Cook for 2–3 minutes on each side while basting fish regularly with butter.

Serve with green olive salsa (page 141).

Sizzling time 5–6 minutes

Serves 4

3 tbsp chopped coriander leaves

2 garlic cloves, crushed

4 tsp ground cumin

4 tsp ground coriander

4 tsp paprika

1 tsp ground turmeric

¹/₃ tsp ground white pepper

¹/₂ tsp salt

2 tsp olive oil

2 tbsp lemon juice

2 small red chillies, finely diced

4 x 200 g (7 oz) firm fish fillets

Mix coriander leaves, garlic, spices, salt, oil,

lemon juice and chillies to form a smooth paste.

marakesh fish fillets
Coat fish fillets with paste.

Place fish on oiled barbecue hotplate.

Cook for 4 minutes, rotating once.

Turn over and cook for a further 3 minutes, rotating once.

Serve with tomato and fresh herb salsa (page 140).

Sizzling time 7 minutes

Serves 4

Toast all seeds and nuts separately until fragrant, either in a dry

frying pan or on a baking tray in a preheated oven 180°C (350°F/gas mark 4).

DUKKAH

Allow to cool then combine and crush roughly

75 g (2¹/₂ oz) sesame seeds

in a mortar and pestle or food processor.

30 g (1 oz) coriander seeds

Add salt to taste. **sardines with dukkah**

30 g (1 oz) cumin seeds

Lay vine leaves out flat. **in vine leaves**

50 g (1³/₄ oz) hazelnuts

Place one sardine, skin side down, at the edge of each leaf.

50 g (1³/₄ oz) almonds

Sprinkle sardine with 1 tsp dukkah.

2 tsp sea salt flakes, or to taste

Carefully roll vine leaves around sardines to cover them completely.

Place vine-wrapped sardines on oiled barbecue grill.

20 vine leaves*

Cook for 2 minutes on each side.

20 boned sardines

≡ Sizzling time 4 minutes

Makes 20

Dukkah can also be served with fresh bread and olive oil.
Dunk bread in oil, then in dukkah. Delicious.

Blend garlic, coriander seeds and chilli, using either

a mortar and pestle or a food processor.

Add lime juice, olive oil, salt and pepper.

Marinate sardine fillets for 1 hour.

Turn sardines occasionally. **tunisian sardines**

1 garlic clove

Cook sardines on oiled barbecue hotplate

2 tsp toasted coriander seeds

for 1 minute on each side.

1 small red chilli, finely diced

■ Sizzling time 2 minutes

1¹/₂ tbsp lime juice

Makes 20

2 tbsp olive oil

Or coat sardines with chermoula (page 47),

Salt and freshly ground black pepper

barbecue and serve with tzaziki (page 142).

20 sardine fillets

Place fish in a dish.

Mix remaining ingredients together.

Marinate fish for 30 minutes.

Place fish on oiled barbecue grill.

caribbean garfish Cook for 3 minutes.

Turn over and cook for a further 3 minutes.

Serve with fresh mango salsa (page 140).

Sizzling time 6 minutes

Serves 4

4 garfish, herring or mullet, cleaned

3 tbsp lime juice

1 tsp allspice

3 spring onions, thinly sliced

1 small red chilli, finely diced

1/2 tsp salt

2 tbsp oil

Place red pepper, chillies, garlic, lemongrass and fish sauce

in food processor and blend until smooth.

thai fish cakes Add fish and process until smooth.

Add coconut milk and egg and mix until combined.

Refrigerate for at least 1 hour, or up to 24 hours.

Form into 20 burger shapes.

Cook on oiled barbecue hotplate for 4–5 minutes on each side.

Serve with coriander pesto (page 143) or sweet chilli sauce (page 145).

Sizzling time 9–10 minutes

Makes 20 small cakes

1 small red pepper, diced

2 red chillies, finely diced

2 garlic cloves, peeled

1 lemongrass stalk, chopped

1 tbsp Thai fish sauce

500 g (1 lb) white fish fillets, roughly diced

125 ml (4 fl oz) coconut milk

1 egg

3 tsp Sichuan pepper*

½ tsp salt

½ tsp five-spice powder

4 x 200 g (7 oz) tuna steaks

Olive oil

Place pepper and salt in a dry pan and cook over a medium heat.

Stir until the salt turns golden, approx 3 minutes.

Crush in a mortar and pestle, or food processor, until very fine.

Sieve to remove husks and stir five-spice through.

Brush tuna with oil and sprinkle on spice mix.

Place tuna on barbecue hotplate.   **spice-coated tuna**

Cook for 4 minutes, rotating once.

Turn over and cook for 4 minutes more, rotating once.

Serve with fennel relish (page 141).

■ Sizzling time 8 minutes

Serves 4

This spice mix is also very good on swordfish steaks and quail.

750 g (1½ lb) tuna

4 tbsp shoyu*

2 tbsp mirin*

2 tsp grated ginger

1 tsp sesame oil

1 tsp caster sugar

12 skewers

Cut tuna into 2 cm (¾ in) chunks.

Mix remaining ingredients together.

Marinate tuna for 30 minutes.

Drain excess marinade.   **tuna teriyaki skewers**

Thread 4 chunks onto each skewer.

Use remaining marinade for basting during cooking.

Place tuna on oiled barbecue hotplate and cook for 2 minutes.

Turn over and cook for a further 2 minutes.

■ Sizzling time 4 minutes

Makes 12 skewers

For rare tuna, cook for 4 minutes, or adjust cooking time

to your taste.

Dice salmon into 2cm (³/₄ in) chunks.

Place mint, spring onions and chillies in a food processor.

minty salmon kebabs Pureé briefly.

Add ginger, sugar, lime juice and oil.

Process until smooth.

Pour over salmon and marinate for 30 minutes.

Thread 4 chunks onto each skewer.

Place salmon on oiled barbecue hotplate and cook for 3 minutes.

Turn over and cook for a further 3 minutes.

Serve with fresh mint and green onion salsa (page 141).

Sizzling time 6 minutes ▮

Makes 10 kebabs

750 g (1¹/₂ lb) salmon fillet, skin removed

A handful mint leaves

4 spring onions, roughly chopped

2 small green chillies, finely diced

1 tsp grated ginger

1 tsp caster sugar

1¹/₂ tbsp lime juice

2 tbsp olive oil

10 skewers

Salmon (and tuna) are best served medium-rare,
as overcooking renders oily fish dry.

Place fish in a dish.

Mix remaining ingredients together.

Marinate salmon for 1 hour, turning once.

soy and ginger salmon Drain salmon well.

Use remaining marinade for basting during cooking.

Place salmon on oiled barbecue grill.

Cook for 4 minutes, rotating once.

Turn over and cook for a further 3 minutes, rotating once.

Sizzling time 7 minutes ≡

Serves 4

4 x 200 g (7 oz) salmon steaks

1 tsp grated ginger

1 small red chilli, finely diced

1 tbsp Indonesian soy sauce*

3 tbsp soy sauce

3 tbsp groundnut oil

1 tsp ground coriander

1 tsp ground cumin

2 tsp paprika

1 tsp ground ginger

1 tsp chilli powder

½ tsp allspice

1 tsp ground white pepper

1 tsp salt

1½ tbsp olive oil

4 x 200 g (7 oz) salmon steaks

Mix spices together with salt and oil to form a smooth paste.

Spread spice paste over flesh side of salmon.

Place salmon on oiled barbecue grill, flesh side down.

Cook for 4 minutes, rotating once. **seven-spice salmon steaks**

Turn over and cook for a further 3 minutes, rotating once.

Serve with fennel relish (page 141).

≡ Sizzling time 7 minutes

Serves 4

This is also good with swordfish steaks or cutlets.

75 g (2²/₃ oz) roasted peanuts

30 g (1 oz) coriander leaves

1 large green chilli

1½ tbsp lime juice

1 tbsp Thai fish sauce

1 tsp grated ginger

1 garlic clove

75 ml (2½ fl oz) groundnut oil

4 x 200 g (7 oz) swordfish steaks

Place peanuts, coriander, chilli, lime juice, fish sauce,

ginger and garlic in food processor.

Process briefly. **swordfish with coriander and peanut pesto**

Slowly add oil to form a smooth paste.

Spread pesto on both sides on the swordfish.

Place swordfish on oiled barbecue hotplate; cook for 4 minutes, rotating once.

Turn over and cook for a further 3 minutes, rotating once.

■ Sizzling time 7 minutes

Serves 4

kasbah fish parcels

Lay foil squares out and place ½ teaspoon of chermoula in the centre of each.

Place one fish fillet on top of chermoula.

Divide tomatoes, coriander and spring onions between each fish.

Top each fish with ½ teaspoon of chermoula.

Fold foil over fish and secure tightly.

Place each parcel on barbecue hotplate and cook for 10 minutes.

Serve with simple bok choy salad (page 134).

Sizzling time 10 minutes ■

Serves 4

4 squares of kitchen foil,
approx 30 cm x 30 cm (12 in x 12 in)
4 tsp chermoula (page 47)
4 x 200 g (7 oz) firm white fish fillets
2 tomatoes, diced
2 tbsp chopped coriander leaves
4 spring onions, thinly sliced

barbecued whole fish

Place lime and ginger slices inside the cavity of each fish.

Slash sides of fish diagonally.

Brush fish with oil.

Rub salt and pepper over skin.

Place fish on oiled barbecue grill.

Cover with lid and cook for 8 minutes, rotating once.

Turn over, cover, and cook for 7 minutes, rotating once.

Serve with Asian coleslaw (page 132) and tamarind dipping sauce (page 143).

Sizzling time 15 minutes ≡

Serves 4

2 limes, sliced
10 cm (4 in) ginger, peeled and sliced
4 x 400 g (13 oz) whole fish, cleaned
Olive oil
2 tsp salt
Freshly ground black pepper

1 bok choy*, cut into long strips

1 red pepper, sliced

1 carrot, shredded

A handful coriander leaves

1 garlic clove, crushed

1 tsp grated ginger

1 tbsp Indonesian soy sauce*

1 whole fish, approx 2 kg (4 lb)

or 4 x 400 g (13 oz) small fish, cleaned

Banana leaves*

banana leaf wrapped whole fish

Mix bok choy, red pepper, carrot and coriander together.

Mix garlic, ginger and kecap manis together, pour over vegetables.

Fill fish cavities with vegetables.

Slash sides of fish diagonally.

Wrap fish in banana leaves.

Cook in kettle barbecue, 1 hour for 2 kg (4 lb) fish, 20 minutes for 400 g (13 oz) fish.

Serve with Thai dipping sauce (page 142).

◓ Sizzling time 1 hour for 2 kg (4 lb) fish or 20 minutes for 400 g (13 oz) fish

Serves 4

Small fish can be cooked on a barbecue grill (page 39).

200g (7 oz) mesquite wood chips, soaked

1 whole salmon or ocean trout,

approx 2–3kg (4–6 lb), cleaned

Piece of kitchen foil 60cm x 30cm

(24 in x 12 in)

whole smoky salmon

Prepare kettle barbecue in the normal manner.

When coals have turned to white ash place smoking chips on top.

Lay whole fish onto foil.

Turn up the edges a little to form a small lip.

Place salmon in barbecue.

Cook for 1 hour, or until it is just cooked through.

◓ Sizzling time 1 hour

Serves 8–10

Cooking a whole salmon in a kettle barbecue with smoking wood chips gives a moist, translucent fish with a hint of smoky flavour.

Banana leaf wrapped whole fish

seafood

[seafood]

The slogan 'throw another shrimp on the barbie' is instantly recognisable as summing up barbecuing. It came from advertisements actor Paul Hogan made to promote Australia as a tourist destination and it was a hit in many countries around the world. Many people prefer to throw the prawns, shell and all, straight on the barbecue. A more refined approach, however, is to peel and devein the prawns, thread onto skewers and marinate them. Other crustaceans can also be cooked on the barbecue: crabs, crayfish, even lobster. For large seafood, kettle cooking is the easiest way to go, but any trolley barbecue with a lid (or wok lid) will create the same effect.

Scallops, squid, octopus and oysters can all be cooked on the barbecue. Oysters do not need to be opened – just put them straight on a hot barbecue grill and the heat will open their shells. Spoon on your favourite sauce and enjoy.

Shellfish can take gutsy flavours, so add chilli, soy sauce, spices and garlic in abundance.

Seafood sizzling times

2–3 minutes	Squid
4 minutes	Prawns
3–4 minutes	Scallops
6–8 minutes	King prawns and small crayfish
20 minutes	Large crayfish and lobster

Chermoula prawns with tzaziki

Peel prawns, removing heads, but leaving tails intact.

Remove intestinal tract (devein).

Thread one prawn on each skewer lengthways through the centre.

prawns with green Place prawns on oiled barbecue grill.

papaya salsa Cook for 2 minutes on each side.

Serve with green papaya salsa.

Sizzling time 4 minutes ☰

Makes 30 skewers

Try prawns with the lime and chilli marinade (page 58).

1 kg (2 lb) raw tiger prawns, approx 30

Green papaya salsa (page 140)

30 skewers

Mix spices with salt, lemon juice and olive oil

to form a smooth paste (chermoula).

Peel prawns, removing heads, but leaving tails intact.

chermoula prawns Remove intestinal tract (devein).

Coat prawns with chermoula and marinate for 30 minutes.

Thread one prawn on each skewer lengthways through the centre.

Cook on an oiled barbecue hotplate for 2 minutes on each side.

Serve with tzaziki (page 142).

Sizzling time 4 minutes ■

Makes 30 skewers

CHERMOULA

2 tsp paprika

1 tsp ground ginger

1 tsp chilli powder

1 tsp ground cumin

1 tsp ground coriander

1 tsp ground white pepper

1/2 tsp ground cardamom

1/2 tsp ground cinnamon

1/2 tsp allspice

1 tsp salt

2 tbsp lemon juice

2 1/2 tbsp olive oil

1 kg (2 lb) raw tiger prawns, approx 30

30 skewers

malaysian curry prawns

2 tbsp Malaysian curry paste

200 ml (7 fl oz) coconut cream

Salt

1 kg (2 lb) raw tiger prawns, approx 30

30 skewers

Place curry paste and coconut cream in a small saucepan.

Bring to the boil.

Simmer for 2–3 minutes and add salt to taste.

Peel prawns, removing heads, but leaving tails intact.

Remove intestinal tract (devein).

Thread one prawn on each skewer lengthways through the centre.

Brush with coconut curry sauce.

Place prawns on oiled barbecue hotplate.

Cook for 2 minutes, basting often.

Turn over and cook for a further 2 minutes, basting often.

■ Sizzling time 4 minutes

Makes 30 skewers

Try Thai, Indian or Burmese curry paste instead of Malaysian.

sizzlin' garlic prawns

500 g (1 lb) raw tiger prawns

2 tbsp olive oil

4 garlic cloves, crushed

1 small red chilli, finely diced

Pinch of saffron threads*, soaked in

1 tbsp boiling water, optional

Peel prawns, removing heads, but leaving tails intact.

Remove intestinal tract (devein).

Place sizzle plate on hot barbecue grill and allow to heat for 10 minutes.

Add oil, garlic and chilli.

Cook for 1–2 minutes until fragrant.

Add prawns and cook for 2 minutes, then turn over.

Add saffron water, if using, and cook for a further 2 minutes.

≡ Sizzling time 5 minutes

Serves 2

Sizzle plates are small cast-iron cooking plates.

Use them to cook and serve food.

1 red pepper

2 tbsp olive oil

100 g (3$\frac{1}{2}$ oz) soft butter

10 basil leaves, finely chopped

Salt and freshly ground black pepper

2 x 250 g (8 oz) crayfish or lobster tails

Rub red pepper with oil and barbecue or roast until skin blisters.

Allow to cool then remove skin and seeds. Dice flesh finely.

Place pepper flesh in a heatproof bowl with butter, basil, salt and pepper.

crayfish with roasted red pepper butter

Place bowl on the side of the barbecue.

Cut shellfish in half lengthways.

Place shellfish flesh side down on oiled barbecue hotplate.

Cook for 10–12 minutes, brush with butter 2–3 times.

Turn over and cook for a further 10 minutes, brush with butter 2–3 times.

Sizzling time 20 minutes ■

Serves 4

Try this recipe with smaller shellfish, such as king prawns, langoustine or tiger prawns.

Ask your fishmonger to open up the crabs and remove the gills.

Use a heavy knife to cut the leg sections into quarters; leave the main shells intact.

Mix chillies, chilli jam, soy sauce and sugar together.

chilli crabs

Toss crabs with sauce.

Place crabs in kettle barbecue.

Cover and cook for 15 minutes.

Sizzling time 15 minutes ◓

Serves 4

4 small cooked crabs,

approx 200–300 g (7–10 oz) each

2 red chillies, finely diced

4 tbsp chilli jam* or sweet chilli sauce

2 tbsp soy sauce

50 g (1$\frac{3}{4}$ oz) brown sugar

2 tsp grated ginger

2 small red chillies, finely diced

100 ml (3⅓ fl oz) mirin*

2 tbsp soy sauce

30 g (1 oz) Thai basil leaves*

4 spring onions, thinly sliced

4 squid tubes, cleaned

1 daikon radish*

200 g (7 oz) salad leaves, washed

Mix ginger, chillies, mirin, soy sauce, Thai basil and spring onions together.

Cut squid into ½ cm (¼ in) rings.

Marinate squid for 30 minutes.

Drain well. **calamari with mirin and thai basil**

Peel and grate daikon, combine with salad leaves.

Divide daikon salad between 4 plates.

Place squid on oiled barbecue grill and cook for 1–2 minutes.

Turn over and cook for a further 1 minute.

Divide squid between salads.

≡ Sizzling time 2–3 minutes

Serves 4

8 kaffir lime leaves*, thinly sliced

2 large green chillies, finely diced

Salt and freshly ground black pepper

2½ tbsp groundnut oil

4 squid tubes, cleaned

3–4 limes, cut in half

20 skewers

Mix kaffir lime leaves, chillies, salt, pepper and oil together.

Cut squid into long strips, **green chilli and kaffir lime**

about 2 cm (¾ in) wide, 10 cm (4 in) long. **calamari skewers**

Marinate squid for 15 minutes.

Thread one strip of squid onto each skewer.

Place squid on oiled barbecue grill and cook for 1 minute.

Turn over and cook for 1 minute.

Squeeze lime juice over calamari to serve.

≡ Sizzling time 2 minutes

Makes 20 skewers

These two octopus recipes use baby octopus, which is marinated then placed in kitchen foil parcels to keep it tender. If you can't find baby octopus, use small squid instead.

100 ml (3¹/₂ fl oz) olive oil

4 small red chillies, finely diced

Heat a saucepan, add oil and chillies and cook briefly.

10 canned anchovy fillets, finely chopped

Add anchovies and cook for 30 seconds.

4 tbsp lemon juice

Add lemon juice, lemon zest, chopped parsley and pepper.

Grated zest of 2 lemons

octopus with lemon
Remove from the heat and allow to cool.

A small handful chopped flat leaf parsley

and parsley
Pour over octopus and marinate overnight.

Freshly ground black pepper

Divide octopus evenly between foil squares and seal tightly.

1 kg (2 lb) baby octopus or squid, cleaned

Place foil parcels in kettle barbecue.

6 squares of kitchen foil 30cm x 30cm

Cook for 20 minutes.

(12 in x 12 in)

Sizzling time 20 minutes ⬒

Serves 6

Mix sugar, soy sauce, lime juice and oils together.

oriental octopus
Pour over octopus and marinate overnight.

40 g (1¹/₃ oz) palm sugar*

Divide octopus evenly between foil squares and seal tightly.

3 tbsp light soy sauce

Place foil parcels in kettle barbecue.

1¹/₂ tbsp lime juice

Cook for 20 minutes.

1 tbsp groundnut oil

Sizzling time 20 minutes ⬒

1 tsp sesame oil

Serves 6

1 kg (2 lb) baby octopus or squid, cleaned

6 squares of kitchen foil 30cm x 30cm

(12 in x 12 in)

SAUCE 1

50 g (1³/₄ oz) caster sugar

125 ml (4 fl oz) rice vinegar

3 tbsp lime juice

2 tbsp Thai fish sauce

1 small red chilli, finely diced

4 shallots, thinly sliced

SAUCE 2

2 tbsp mirin*

1 tbsp sweet chilli sauce

1 tbsp light soy sauce

1 tbsp Thai fish sauce

2 spring onions, thinly sliced

6 mint leaves, thinly sliced

2 dozen oysters, still closed in their shells

Sauce 1 – Dissolve sugar in rice vinegar in a small saucepan over a low heat.

When cool add lime juice, fish sauce, chilli and shallots.

Sauce 2 – Mix all ingredients together in a bowl.

oysters two ways

Place oysters on hot barbecue grill (they sit well on the bars).

Cook for 2 minutes, or until the shells pop open.

Using a small knife, pry top shells off and place oysters on a platter.

Spoon either sauce 1 or 2 into shells to serve.

≡ Sizzling time 2–3 minutes

Makes 2 dozen

Try oysters and scallops cooked on the shell with

fresh mint and green onion salsa (page 141).

100g (3¹/₂ oz) soft butter

Freshly ground black pepper

Grated zest of 1 lime

2 tsp grated ginger

1¹/₂ tsp wasabi paste*

Greaseproof paper

2 dozen scallops, cleaned
and attached to their shells

Mix butter, pepper, lime zest, ginger and wasabi paste together.

Place on a sheet of greaseproof paper and roll into a tube shape.

Chill until needed. **scallops with wasabi and ginger butter**

Cut hardened butter into thin slices, and keep on ice.

Place scallops on hot barbecue grill, shell side down.

Cover with a lid or foil and cook for 2–3 minutes.

To serve, place a slice of butter on top of each scallop.

≡ Sizzling time 3 minutes

Makes 24

Discard shellfish if the shells are open before cooking, and any that do not open during cooking.

Thread one end of a bacon rasher onto a skewer.

Add a scallop, wrap bacon around scallop.

Add another scallop, wrap bacon around then add a final scallop.

bacon and scallop skewers Grind pepper over skewers.

Place skewers on oiled barbecue grill.

Cook for 4–5 minutes, turning 2–3 times.

Sizzling time 4 minutes

Makes 10

10 thin slices streaky bacon

500 g (1 lb) scallops, cleaned

Freshly ground black pepper

10 skewers

poultry and game

[poultry and game]

From simple barbecued chicken fillets to more complex marinades for quail, duck and turkey, poultry offers something for all tastes. Chicken wings, drumsticks, drumlets (the meatiest pieces from the wing), breasts and whole chickens can all be cooked successfully on the barbecue. Chicken thighs are particularly good for barbecuing. They have only one bone remaining, making them easy to cook and juicy to eat. A free-range or grain-fed chicken will have much more flavour, but these can be hard to find in some of the smaller cuts.

Whole chickens and smaller pieces with bones intact often need to be cooked with a lid (such as a wok lid or a piece of kitchen foil). This speeds up the cooking time and helps to keep the moisture in, preventing the chicken turning out dry. Spatchcocking a bird is simply cutting through the backbone and pressing it out flat. This allows large cuts of poultry to be cooked in about 40 minutes.

Chicken goes well with simple flavours such as herbs, butter, olive oil and lemon, with heartier flavours like chillies, spices and soy sauce as well as Indian, Italian, Mexican and Middle-Eastern style marinades.

Poultry and game sizzling times

10–12 minutes	Breast fillets
15 minutes	Boneless thigh fillets
20 minutes	Chicken thighs
15–20 minutes	Wings and drumlets
30 minutes	Drumsticks
35–40 minutes	Spatchcocked chickens
8–10 minutes	Spatchcocked quails
30 minutes	Spatchcocked poussin (small chicken)
20 minutes	Duck breast fillets
40 minutes	Spatchcocked ducks
2 hours	Turkey (with legs removed; see page 66)

To spatchcock a bird, insert a sharp knife into the cavity. Hold the knife point and cut through, pressing down firmly. Trim back bone away and any excess skin. Press bird flat. If preferred, trim rib bones and you're ready to go.

3 tbsp olive oil

3 tbsp chopped herbs

Salt and freshly ground black pepper

4 chicken breast fillets, skinned

Mix oil, herbs, salt and pepper together.

Marinate chicken for 2 hours.

simple herb chicken fillets   Drain excess marinade.

Use remaining marinade for basting during cooking.

Place chicken on oiled barbecue grill.

Cook for 6 minutes, rotating once.

Turn over and cook for a further 4–6 minutes, rotating once.

Serve with roast red pepper relish (page 144).

Sizzling time 10–12 minutes ≡

Serves 4

3 tbsp balsamic vinegar

2 tsp brown sugar

1 tbsp olive oil

Salt and freshly ground black pepper

4 chicken breast fillets, skinned

Mix vinegar and sugar together, add oil, salt and pepper.

Marinate chicken for 1 hour.

balsamic chicken fillets   Drain excess marinade.

Use remaining marinade for basting during cooking.

Place chicken on oiled barbecue grill.

Cook for 6 minutes, rotating once.

Turn over and cook for a further 4–6 minutes, rotating once.

Sizzling time 10–12 minutes ≡

Serves 4

Balsamic marinade gives the chicken a blackened

appearance and a wonderful sweet-sour flavour.

8 chicken drumsticks

2 garlic cloves, crushed

2 tsp ground coriander

2 tsp ground cumin

½ tsp paprika

3 tsp chopped parsley leaves

½ tsp salt

2½ tbsp lemon juice

3 tbsp olive oil

Place chicken in a dish.

Mix remaining ingredients together.

Marinate chicken for 30 minutes. **spicy lip-smacking**

Place chicken on barbecue hotplate. **drumsticks**

Cook for 30 minutes, turning often.

■ Sizzling time 30 minutes

Serves 4

Mix lime juice, chilli, salt, sugar and oil together.

Marinate chicken for 1 hour.

Drain excess marinade. **lime and chilli chicken wings**

LIME AND CHILLI MARINADE

125 ml (4 fl oz) lime juice

4 small red chillies, finely diced

½ tsp salt

1 tsp caster sugar

3 tbsp olive oil

Use remaining marinade for basting during cooking.

Place chicken on oiled barbecue grill.

Cook for 20 minutes, turning often.

≡ Sizzling time 20 minutes

Serves 5–6

Try lime and chilli marinade on prawns or lamb cutlets.

1 kg (2 lb) chicken wings

1 garlic clove, crushed

1/2 tsp salt

1/2 tsp chilli powder

1 tsp paprika

1/2 tsp ground coriander

1/2 tsp ground cumin

1/2 tsp freshly ground black pepper

1 tsp yellow mustard seeds, crushed

1 tbsp olive oil

1 kg (2 lb) chicken drumlets (the meatiest

pieces from the wings)

mexican spicy drumlets

Mix garlic, salt, spices, mustard seeds and oil together.

Rub over chicken.

Place chicken on oiled barbecue grill.

Cook for 20 minutes, turning often.

Sizzling time 20 minutes ≡

Serves 5–6

1 kg (2 lb) chicken wings

125 ml (4 fl oz) soy sauce

1 tbsp Worcestershire sauce

2 tbsp honey

2 1/2 tbsp tomato ketchup

blackened chicken wings

Place chicken in a bowl.

Mix remaining ingredients together.

Marinate chicken for 1 hour.

Drain excess marinade.

Use remaining marinade for basting during cooking.

Place chicken on oiled barbecue grill.

Cook for 20 minutes, turning often.

Sizzling time 20 minutes ≡

Serves 5–6

Lip-smacking, Mexican spicy
and blackened chicken recipes
can be used on any cut of
chicken: drumlets, wings,
drumsticks, thighs or breasts.

fig and chicken salad

2 chicken breast fillets, skinned

Olive oil for cooking

4 figs, cut in half

1 round-headed lettuce, washed

150 g (5 oz) rocket leaves, washed

100 g (3½ oz) feta cheese, diced

100 g (3½ oz) Kalamata olives

1 avocado, sliced

60 g (2 oz) cherry tomatoes, halved

12 basil leaves, torn

1 tbsp lemon juice

1 tbsp runny honey

100 ml (3½ fl oz) olive oil

Salt and freshly ground black pepper

Brush chicken fillets with olive oil.

Place chicken on oiled barbecue grill.

Cook for 6 minutes, rotating once.

Turn over and cook for a further 4–6 minutes, rotating once.

Add figs flesh side down for the last minute of cooking.

Mix together lettuce, rocket, feta, olives, avocado,

cherry tomatoes and basil leaves.

Mix together lemon juice, honey and olive oil.

Season to taste.

Slice chicken and place on top of salad.

Arrange figs around and pour dressing over.

Sizzling time 10 minutes

Serves 4

chicken saltimbocca skewers

Mix together oil, sage, salt and pepper.

Cut each chicken fillet into 6 long strips.

Mix sage oil and chicken together.

Cut prosciutto slices in half lengthways.

Lay 1 slice of prosciutto flat and place 1 strip of chicken on top.

Thread prosciutto and chicken onto skewers.

Place chicken on oiled barbecue hotplate.

Cook for 4 minutes on each side.

Sizzling time 8 minutes

Makes 24

2 tbsp olive oil

2 tbsp chopped fresh sage

Salt and freshly ground black pepper

4 chicken breast fillets, skinned

12 thin slices prosciutto*

24 skewers

Place lemongrass and onion in food processor and purée.

Add garlic and ginger, purée again.

Add chillies and coriander and purée briefly.

Add fish sauce and just enough oil to form a smooth paste.

Cut chicken into 2 cm ($^3/_4$ in) chunks.

chicken and lemongrass skewers
Marinate chicken for 30 minutes.

Thread 4–5 pieces chicken onto each skewer.

Place chicken on oiled barbecue grill.

Cook for 8–10 minutes, turning 3–4 times.

Sizzling time 10 minutes ≡

Makes 16

1 lemongrass* stem, chopped

$^1/_2$ onion, chopped

1 garlic clove, peeled

2 cm ($^3/_4$ in) ginger, peeled and chopped

2 green chillies, finely diced

30 g (1 oz) coriander leaves

1 tbsp Thai fish sauce

2$^1/_2$ tbsp groundnut oil

4 chicken breast fillets, skinned

16 skewers

Make sure all the ingredients are finely chopped before adding to the food processor. This makes them easier to purée and saves the machine's motor.

1 kg (2 lb) chicken mince

2 tsp grated ginger

2 tbsp sweet chilli sauce

2 tbsp Indonesian soy sauce*

80 g (2$^3/_4$ oz) breadcrumbs

Mix all ingredients together.

Divide mixture into 20 portions.

ginger-chicken burgers
Form into burger shapes.

Place chicken on oiled barbecue hotplate.

Cook for 4 minutes, rotating once.

Turn over and cook for a further 3–4 minutes, rotating once.

Serve with satay sauce (page 143).

Sizzling time 8 minutes ▰

Makes 20 burgers

Finely chop black beans.

Mix black beans with chilli paste and kecap manis.

1 tbsp black beans*, soaked and drained

Cut each thigh fillet into 4 even-sized pieces.

1 tsp chilli paste

Marinate chicken for 1 hour. **pandan chicken parcels**

1 tbsp Indonesian soy sauce*

Place one piece of chicken at one end of each leaf.

1 kg (2 lb) boneless chicken thighs, skinned

Roll leaf around chicken.

24 pandan leaves*, banana leaves or

Secure leaf with a toothpick through the chicken.

squares of kitchen foil

Place chicken parcels on oiled barbecue grill.

Toothpicks

Cook chicken for 10–12 minutes, turning regularly.

≡ Sizzling time 12 minutes

Makes 24 parcels

Mix together butter, garlic, herbs, salt and pepper.

Place garlic butter in heatproof bowl and put on side of the barbecue.

Pull leaves back on corn cobs and remove silky tassels. **garlic-basted**

GARLIC BUTTER

Smear each cob with extra butter and roll leaves back up. **chicken and corn**

100 g (3½ oz) soft butter

Place chicken on oiled barbecue grill and brush with garlic butter.

2 garlic cloves, crushed

Cook chicken for 20 minutes, rotating once.

3 tbsp chopped herbs

Place corn cobs on barbecue grill 10 minutes after the chicken, turn regularly.

Salt and freshly ground black pepper

Turn chicken over, cook for 20 minutes, rotating once.

≡ Sizzling time 40 minutes

4 corn cobs

Serves 4

30 g (1 oz) extra butter

4 chicken thighs

Chicken saltimbocca skewers

Spiced lamb kebabs

4 boneless chicken thighs, skinned

250 g (8 oz) natural yoghurt

2 tbsp tandoori paste

1 tbsp lemon juice

12 skewers

2 tomatoes, finely diced

Dice chicken into 2 cm (¾ in) chunks.

Mix together yoghurt, tandoori paste and lemon juice.

Marinate chicken for 1 hour.

½ cucumber, finely diced

chicken tandoori
Thread 4–5 pieces of chicken onto each skewer.

2 spring onions, thinly sliced

in indian bread
Place chicken on barbecue hotplate.

1 tbsp chopped mint

Cook for 12 minutes, turning 3–4 times.

Mix together tomato, cucumber, spring onion, mint, additional juice and oil.

1 tbsp lemon juice, additional

Place bread on oiled barbecue grill for 1–2 minutes before serving.

2 tbsp olive oil

Serve skewers in hot bread with salad over the top.

4 roti bread or Indian bread (page 26)

Add additional natural yoghurt.

Natural yoghurt, additional

Sizzling time 12 minutes ■ ≡

Serves 4

Place poussins in a dish.

Place remaining ingredients in a food processor.

4 x 250 g (8 oz) poussin, spatchcocked

indonesian marinated poussin
Process until smooth.

4 garlic cloves, crushed

Marinate poussins for 1 hour.

4 spring onions, thinly sliced

Place poussins on oiled barbecue grill, cover with lid.

60 g (2 oz) brown sugar

Cook for 15 minutes, rotating 2–3 times.

2½ tbsp lemon juice

Turn over and cover with a lid.

2 green chillies

Cook for a further 15 minutes, rotating 2–3 times.

3 tbsp soy sauce

Cut in half along breastbone to serve.

1 tsp ground turmeric

Serve with Asian coleslaw (page 132).

2 tsp ground coriander

Sizzling time 30 minutes ≡

2 tsp grated fresh ginger

Serves 4

100 g (3½ oz) peanuts, ground

100 ml (3½ fl oz) olive oil

1 x 1.6 kg (3 lb) chicken, spatchcocked

2 garlic cloves, crushed

A handful chopped herbs – mix of parsley,

thyme, basil and oregano

1 tbsp lemon juice

Salt and freshly ground black pepper

Pinch of ground cumin

Pinch of ground coriander

Pinch of paprika

2$^1/_2$ tbsp olive oil

Place chicken in a flat dish.

Mix remaining ingredients together.

Brush chicken all over with herb mixture.

Place chicken on oiled barbecue hotplate, cover with lid.

Cook for 15 minutes, rotating 2–3 times.

Turn over and cover with lid. **whole barbecued chicken**

Cook for a further 15 minutes, rotating 2–3 times. **with lemon and herbs**

Remove lid, baste well and continue cooking for 10 minutes.

■ Sizzling time 40 minutes

Serves 4

Try this method with different marinades,

such as Oriental (page 16) or Kashmiri marinade (opposite).

1 turkey with legs removed, 3.5–4 kg (7–8 lb)

4 tsp ground cumin

4 tsp ground coriander

2 tsp ground ginger

2 pinches saffron threads*, approx 20

$^1/_2$ tsp ground cinnamon

Pinch of ground cloves

$^1/_3$ tsp freshly ground black pepper

$^1/_2$ tsp salt

2$^1/_2$ tbsp olive oil

Pat turkey dry.

Mix spices together with salt and oil.

Brush spice mixture over the turkey skin.

Place turkey on a baking tray and into a kettle barbecue.

Cook for 2 hours in total. **moroccan barbecued turkey**

Remove and rest for 20 minutes before carving.

◒ Sizzling time 2 hours

Serves 12

By removing the turkey's legs, the bird will take less time to cook than a whole turkey and has white meat only.

KASHMIRI MARINADE

100 g (3½ oz) natural yoghurt

1 tsp grated ginger

Mix yoghurt with ginger, garlic, lemon juice, spices, salt and oil.

1 garlic clove, crushed

kashmiri quail   Marinate quails for 2 hours.

2 tsp lemon juice

Place quail on oiled barbecue grill.

1 tsp ground cumin

Cook for 5 minutes, rotating once.

⅓ tsp ground white pepper

Turn over and cook for a further 5 minutes, rotating once.

½ tsp ground turmeric

Cut in half along breastbone to serve.

½ tsp chilli powder

Sizzling time 10 minutes ≡

⅓ tsp ground cinnamon

Serves 4–6

½ tsp salt

1 tbsp olive oil

6 quails, spatchcocked

Place pepper and salt in a dry pan and cook over a medium heat.

Stir until the salt turns golden, approx 3 minutes.

Crush in a mortar and pestle, or food processor until very fine.

Sieve to remove husks and stir five-spice through.

salt and pepper quail   Brush quail skins with oil.

3 tsp Sichuan pepper*

Sprinkle with salt and pepper mix.

½ tsp salt

Place quail on oiled barbecue grill.

½ tsp five-spice powder

Cook for 4–5 minutes, rotating once.

6 quails, spatchcocked

Turn over and cook for a further 4 minutes, rotating once.

Olive oil

Cut in half along breastbone to serve.

Sizzling time 8–9 minutes ≡

Serves 4–6

Try quail with pomegranate marinade (page 69).

2 tbsp lemon juice

3 tsp ground cumin

1 tsp toasted cumin seeds

1 tsp caster sugar

½ tsp salt

1 tsp harissa*

2½ tbsp olive oil

6 quails, spatchcocked

Mix lemon juice, spices, sugar, salt, harissa and oil together.

Marinate quails for 30 minutes. **quail with cumin crust**

Place quail on oiled barbecue grill.

Cook for 4–5 minutes, rotating once.

Turn over and cook for a further 4 minutes, rotating once.

Cut in half along breastbone to serve.

Sizzling time 8–9 minutes

Serves 4–6

Good with babaganoush (page 24).

Place duck breasts skin side down on oiled barbecue grill.

Baste with plum sauce. **duck with plum sauce**

Cook for 9–10 minutes, rotating 1–2 times.

Turn over and cook for a further 8–9 minutes, rotating 1–2 times.

Rest for 5 minutes.

Slice thickly to serve.

Serve with remaining plum sauce.

4 boneless duck breasts

250 ml (8 fl oz) plum and ginger sauce

(page 146), or bottled plum sauce

Sizzling time 17–19 minutes

Serves 4

pomegranate and sumac glazed duck

Combine syrup, oil, sumac, salt and pepper.

Marinate duck for 1 hour.

Drain excess marinade.

Use remaining marinade for basting during cooking.

Place duck breasts skin side down on oiled barbecue grill.

Cook for 9–10 minutes, rotating 1–2 times.

Turn over and cook for a further 8–9 minutes, rotating 1–2 times.

Rest for 5 minutes.

Slice thickly to serve.

Sizzling time 17–19 minutes ≡

Serves 4

POMEGRANATE MARINADE

4 tbsp pomegranate syrup*

1$^1/_2$ tbsp olive oil

3 tsp sumac*

Salt and freshly ground black pepper

4 boneless duck breasts

japanese glazed duck

Trim excess fat and skin from duck.

Place duck in a shallow dish.

Mix remaining ingredients together.

Marinate duck for 2 hours.

Drain excess marinade.

Use remaining marinade for basting during cooking.

Place duck on medium-heat oiled barbecue hotplate.

Cook for 10 minutes, rotating once.

Cover and cook for a further 10 minutes.

Turn duck over and cook uncovered for 10 minutes, rotating once.

Cover and cook for a final 10 minutes.

Rest for 5 minutes.

Cut into 4 portions to serve.

Sizzling time 40 minutes ■

Serves 4

1 x 2 kg (4 lb) duck, spatchcocked

3 tbsp tamari*

1 tsp sesame oil

1 tbsp mirin*

3 tbsp orange juice

20 g (²/₃ oz) jasmine tea

2 star anise

250 ml (8 fl oz) boiling water

80 g (2³/₄ oz) honey

10 cm (4 in) ginger, peeled and

cut into matchsticks

1 x 2 kg (4 lb) duck, spatchcocked

Combine tea and star anise and pour boiling water over.

Allow to brew for 5 minutes, then strain. Allow tea to cool.

Mix tea, honey and ginger together.

Marinate duck for 4 hours.

Drain excess marinade. **tea-scented sticky duck**

Use remaining marinade for basting during cooking.

Place duck on medium-heat oiled barbecue hotplate.

Cook for 10 minutes, rotating once.

Cover and cook for a further 10 minutes.

Turn duck over and cook uncovered for 10 minutes, rotating once.

Cover and cook for a final 10 minutes.

Rest for 5 minutes.

Cut into 4 portions to serve.

■ Sizzling time 40 minutes

Serves 4

1 kg (2 lb) kangaroo or venison

1 tbsp red wine

1 tbsp olive oil

1 tsp salt

4 tsp freshly ground black pepper

12 skewers

Dice meat into 2 cm (³/₄ in) chunks.

Mix meat, red wine and oil together.

Marinate meat for 30 minutes. **peppered kangaroo kebabs**

Thread meat onto skewers, sprinkle with salt and pepper.

Cook on hot oiled barbecue grill for 8 minutes, turning 3–4 times.

Rest for 5 minutes.

≡ Sizzling time 8 minutes

Makes 12 kebabs

Try kangaroo if you can get it, otherwise use venison fillet.

beef

A perfectly cooked steak, seared on the surface and packed with pink juices, is second to none. The barbecue could, in fact, have been made just for cooking the perfect steak. Personal preference dictates cut of steak and the degree of cooking. Choose traditionally prepared beef when possible for a fuller flavour and more succulent meat.

Allow steaks to come to room temperature before cooking. A good steak needs little adornment. If you must add something, keep it simple such as pepper, chilli or mustard. The worst thing you can do to your steak is to overcook it. Experience will teach you how well the steak is cooked.

It goes without saying, but don't flip-flop the meat around.

Other than mastering the cooking time, it is also important to let steak rest before serving. Rest in a warm place away from direct heat, such as the side of the barbecue, in a warm oven or between two plates and wrapped in a tea towel. Beware of strong winds if outside. This window of opportunity also gives you a few minutes to collect the forgotten things and dress the salad.

Remember, if you learn nothing else from Sizzle! but how to cook the perfect steak on the barbecue, you have learnt the best lesson of all.

Beef sizzling times

10 minutes	Sirloin	2.5 cm (1 in), 200 g (7 oz)
10 minutes	Rump	2 cm ($^3/_4$ in)
12 minutes	T-bone	400 g (13 oz)
18 minutes	Fillet	5 cm (2 in)
20 minutes	Rib of beef	400 g (13 oz)
30 minutes	Whole fillet	1.5 kg (3 lb)

HOW WELL COOKED IS YOUR STEAK?

Prod it to find out…
- *Raw* it's almost like soft butter
- *Rare* it's like a sponge
- *Medium-rare* the steak should feel like the fleshier base of your thumb
- *Medium* like your middle finger
- *Well done* it can bounce.

THE PERFECT SIRLOIN

Sirloin steak is one of the more tender cuts available. It offers a good balance between flavour and juiciness, with just a thin layer of fat across the top to keep it moist during cooking.

Place sirloin steak on oiled barbecue grill.

Cook for 6 minutes, rotating once.

Turn over and cook for a further 4–5 minutes, rotating once.

Rest for 5 minutes.

≡ Sizzling time for medium-rare steak 10 minutes, 12 for medium

NB Thicker or heavier steaks will take longer to cook.

THE PERFECT RUMP

Rump steak may not be as tender as other steaks, but it is gutsy, full-flavoured meat that is perfectly suited to barbecuing. Rump steaks often weigh up to 500 g (1 lb) each and may need to be cut in half for a regular portion.

Place rump steak on oiled barbecue grill.

Cook for 6 minutes, rotating once.

Turn over and cook for a further 4–5 minutes, rotating once.

Rest for 5 minutes.

≡ Sizzling time 10 minutes

THE PERFECT T-BONE

T-bone steak is meat for a big appetite, often weighing in at 400–500 g (¾ –1 lb).

With the distinctive T-shaped bone down the centre, it has sirloin on one side and fillet on the other.

Place T-bone steak on oiled barbecue grill.

Cook for 6 minutes, rotating once.

Turn over and cook for a further 5–6 minutes, rotating once.

Rest for 5 minutes.

≡ Sizzling time 12 minutes

THE PERFECT FILLET

Fillet steak, sometimes known as eye fillet, is the prime cut from beef, with negligible visible fat, no waste and is incredibly tender.

Flavour is neither too mild nor too strong. Fillet steak is often up to 7 cm (2¾ in) thick and will need a longer cooking time than other steaks.

Place fillet steak on oiled barbecue grill.

Cook for 10 minutes, rotating once.

Turn over and cook for a further 8 minutes, rotating once.

Rest for 5 minutes.

≡ Sizzling time 18 minutes

NB Thin fillet steaks will take less time to cook.

VARIATIONS

Mustard steak – rub with Dijon or wholegrain mustard.

Chilli steak – rub steaks with chilli paste (add as much as you can tolerate).

Pepper steak – cover steaks with lashings of freshly ground black pepper (or crushed green peppercorns).

Garlic steak – baste steak with garlic butter (page 62) during cooking.

SERVE STEAK WITH...

Garlic mushrooms (page 123)
Barbecued onion rings (page 122)
Potato wedges (page 125)
Green salad (page 128)
Sage and walnut mustard (page 147).

rib of beef with anchovy butter

ANCHOVY BUTTER

100 g (3½ oz) soft butter

25 g (¾ oz) canned anchovy fillets

Freshly ground black pepper

1 tbsp lemon juice

Grated zest of 1 lemon

1 tbsp chopped parsley leaves

4 ribs of beef, approx 400 g (13 oz) each

1–2 tbsp olive oil

Freshly ground black pepper

Prepare anchovy butter by mixing all the ingredients together.

Place on a square piece of greaseproof paper.

Roll paper to form a sausage shape and refrigerate.

Rub beef with olive oil and sprinkle with pepper.

Place ribs on oiled barbecue grill.

Cook for 10 minutes, rotating 1–2 times.

Turn over and cook for further 9–10 minutes, rotating 1–2 times.

Rest beef for 10 minutes.

Remove paper from butter and slice thickly.

Add one or two slices of butter to each rib and serve.

≡ Sizzling time 20–25 minutes

Serves 4

NB The thickness of the ribs will affect the cooking time.

fillet with chilli and garlic marinade

1 large red chilli, finely diced

2 garlic cloves, crushed

1 tsp freshly ground black pepper

½ tsp sea salt

125 ml (4 fl oz) olive oil

1 fillet of beef, approx 1.5 kg (3 lb)

Mix chilli, garlic, pepper, salt and oil together.

Marinate beef for 30 minutes.

Drain well.

Use remaining marinade for basting during cooking.

Place fillet on oiled barbecue grill.

Cook for 8–10 minutes on each side, rolling fillet over as required.

Rest for 15 minutes before slicing.

≡ Sizzling time 30 minutes for rare meat

≡ Sizzling time 40 minutes for medium meat

Serves 6–8

Cut beef into 2 cm (¾ in) chunks.

Mix mustard, rosemary, oil, red wine, salt and pepper together.

classic beef and mushroom kebabs   Marinate beef for 1 hour.

Cut red pepper in half, remove seeds and dice to 2 cm (¾ in).

Wipe mushrooms clean and cut in half.

Drain excess marinade.

Thread beef, mushrooms and red pepper onto skewers.

Use remaining marinade for basting during cooking.

Place kebabs on oiled barbecue grill.

Cook for 12 minutes, turning 3–4 times.

Sizzling time 12 minutes ≡

Makes 14 kebabs

Use fresh rosemary branches instead
of skewers to add more flavour.

1 kg (2 lb) tender beef, such as fillet,

sirloin or rump

2 tsp Dijon mustard

2 tsp chopped fresh rosemary

2 tbsp olive oil

3 tbsp red wine

Salt and freshly ground black pepper

1 red pepper

14 button mushrooms

14 skewers

Cut beef into 1 cm (½ in) chunks.

Place remaining ingredients in the food processor.

beef satay kebabs   Blend until smooth.

Marinate beef for 1 hour.

Thread 4–5 pieces of beef on each skewer.

Place beef skewers on oiled barbecue grill.

Cook for 5 minutes, turning 2–3 times.

Sizzling time 5 minutes ≡

Makes 20 small skewers

500 g (1 lb) tender beef, such as fillet,

sirloin or rump

1 small onion, diced

1 tbsp soy sauce

3 tbsp groundnut oil

2 tsp ground coriander

1 tsp ground cumin

1 tsp ground turmeric

⅓ tsp ground cinnamon

1 tsp salt

1 tsp sugar

50 g (1¾ oz) roasted peanuts

20 skewers

1 onion, diced

1 red pepper, diced

1 courgette, diced

1 aubergine, diced

100 ml (3½ fl oz) olive oil

Salt and freshly ground black pepper

1 kg (2 lb) beef mince

Place diced vegetables in a baking tray and toss with oil.

Roast in a preheated 180°C (350°F/gas mark 4) oven for 30–40 minutes, stirring often.

When cool, mix vegetables with beef mince.

Season with salt and pepper. **beef burgers with roasted vegetables**

Divide into 8 portions and form into burger shapes.

Place burgers on oiled barbecue grill.

Cook for 4 minutes, rotating once.

Turn over; cook for a further 3–4 minutes, rotating once.

For a medium burger, cook for another 2 minutes.

≡ Sizzling time 7–8 minutes

Makes 8

500 g (1 lb) beef mince

½ tsp ground nutmeg

½ tsp ground cinnamon

1 tsp ground coriander

1 tsp ground cumin

1 tbsp chopped mint leaves

1 tbsp chopped coriander leaves

⅓ tsp salt

⅓ tsp freshly ground black pepper

50 large basil leaves

10 skewers

Mix beef, spices and herbs (except basil leaves) together with salt and pepper.

Take a heaped teaspoonful of the mixture and roll into a ball.

Repeat to make 50 balls.

Wrap each ball in a basil leaf. **spiced beef in basil leaves**

Skewer 5 basil-wrapped meatballs onto each skewer.

Place skewers on oiled barbecue grill.

Cook for 8 minutes, turning 3–4 times.

≡ Sizzling time 8 minutes

Makes 10 skewers

2 tbsp shoyu*

1 tbsp mirin*

1 tsp grated ginger

6 x 100 g (3½ oz) fillet steaks

Mix shoyu, mirin and ginger together.

Marinate beef for 30 minutes.

Drain excess marinade. **shoyu beef**

Place beef on oiled barbecue grill.

Cook for 2 minutes, rotating once.

Turn over; cook for 2 minutes, rotating once.

Remove, rest briefly and serve.

≡ Sizzling time 4 minutes

Makes 6 small steaks

6 x 100 g (3½ oz) fillet steaks

2 tbsp soy sauce

2 tsp sesame oil

3 tsp bean paste* or miso*

2 tbsp rice wine*

1 tsp toasted sesame seeds

2 tsp chilli paste

1 garlic clove, crushed

Place beef in a bowl.

Mix remaining ingredients together.

Marinate beef for 30 minutes.

Drain excess marinade. **korean fiery beef**

Place beef on oiled barbecue grill.

Cook for 2 minutes, rotating once.

Turn over; cook for 2 minutes, rotating once.

Remove, rest briefly and serve.

≡ Sizzling time 4 minutes

Makes 6 small steaks

Spiced beef in basil leaves

veal and roasted pepper burgers

Combine all ingredients well.

Divide into 8 and form into burger shapes.

Place burgers on oiled barbecue grill.

Cook for 4 minutes, rotating once.

Turn over and cook for a further 4 minutes, rotating once.

Sizzling time 8 minutes ≡

Makes 8 burgers

500 g (1 lb) veal mince

1 roasted red pepper, peeled, deseeded and diced

50 g (1¾ oz) pine nuts, toasted

2 tbsp chopped basil leaves

1 tbsp tomato purée

Salt and freshly ground black pepper

veal cutlets with maple syrup and mustard glaze

Mix syrup, mustard, salt and pepper together.

Place cutlets on oiled barbecue grill.

Baste often with glaze.

Cook for 10 minutes, rotating once.

Turn over and cook for a further 8–10 minutes, basting often.

Rest for 5 minutes.

Sizzling time 18–20 minutes ≡

Serves 4

2 tbsp maple syrup

3 tsp Dijon mustard

Salt and freshly ground black pepper

4 x 300 g (10½ oz) veal cutlets

marinated liver and bacon kebabs

Combine garlic, oil, sage and pepper together.

Marinate liver for 1 hour.

Thread liver onto skewers, placing a piece of bacon between each cube.

Place skewers on oiled barbecue grill or hotplate.

Cook for 4–5 minutes, turning 2–3 times.

Serve with lemon wedges.

Sizzling time 4–5 minutes ≡■

Makes 10 skewers

2 garlic cloves, crushed

1½ tbsp olive oil

10 sage leaves, finely chopped

Freshly ground black pepper

400 g (13 oz) calves' liver, cut into 2 cm (¾ in) cubes

2–3 bacon rashers, cut into 2 cm (¾ in) pieces

2 lemons, cut into wedges

10 skewers

lamb

[lamb]

Lamb, unfortunately, has a tendency to be fatty. Luckily for us, lean lamb is now readily available and lamb topside, loin, steaks and trimmed cutlets are a revelation. This lamb is excellent for barbecuing and can take lots of extra flavours through marinating and basting.

Prime cuts of lamb, like beef, are used most for barbecuing. These are cuts from the rear quarter, which cook quickly and should be served medium-rare to be enjoyed at their best. Experiment with the different cuts available, or go all the way and try a spit-roasted whole lamb. If you have ever been lucky enough to attend a barbecue where a spit-roasted lamb (studded with garlic and rosemary) was cooked, you know just how good lamb can be. If you haven't, give it a go this summer.

Delicious Mediterranean, Middle-Eastern and Asian influences dominate the dishes in this chapter. Always remember, however, there is nothing quite as satisfying as simple yet perfectly barbecued lamb cutlets.

Lamb sizzling times

4 minutes Lamb steaks

6 minutes Fillets (tenderloin)

8 minutes Trimmed cutlets

8 minutes Loin

12 minutes Whole topside

30 minutes Leg (boned and laid flat)

3 hours Spit-roasted lamb

Rub lamb with oil, salt and pepper.

Place lamb on oiled barbecue grill.

Cook for 4 minutes, rotating once.

Turn lamb over and cook for 3–4 minutes, rotating once.

simple barbecued lamb   Rest for 5 minutes.

Slice thickly and serve with barbecued polenta (page 116).

Sizzling time 7–8 minutes ≡

Serves 4

4 lamb loins

Olive oil

Salt and freshly ground black pepper

Dice lamb into 2 cm (³/₄ in) squares.

Mix remaining ingredients together.

rosemary lamb kebabs   Marinate lamb for 2 hours.

Thread lamb onto skewers, approx 6 pieces per skewer.

Use remaining marinade for basting during cooking.

Place lamb on oiled barbecue hotplate.

Cook for 6 minutes turning 3–4 times.

Serve with tomato and white bean salad (page 130).

Sizzling time 6 minutes ■

Makes 20 skewers

For an extra rosemary flavour, thread lamb onto rosemary branches.

8 lamb fillets

75 ml (2¹/₂ fl oz) olive oil

1 tbsp lemon juice

2 tbsp chopped fresh rosemary

Salt and freshly ground black pepper

20 skewers

1 tsp paprika

1 tsp ground cumin

1 tsp ground coriander

½ tsp salt

1 tbsp lemon juice

2 tbsp olive oil

8 lamb fillets

20 skewers

Mix together spices, salt, lemon juice and olive oil.

Dice lamb into 2 cm (¾ in) squares.

Marinate lamb for 1 hour. **spiced lamb kebabs**

Thread lamb onto skewers, approx 6 pieces per skewer.

Place lamb on oiled barbecue hotplate.

Cook for 6 minutes, turning 3–4 times.

Serve with tzaziki (page 142) and watercress tabouleh (page 130).

▪ Sizzling time 6 minutes

Makes 20

40 g (1⅓ oz) caster sugar

1½ tbsp lime juice

3 tbsp soy sauce

2 small red chillies, finely diced

1 tbsp groundnut oil

16 lean lamb cutlets

Dissolve sugar in lime juice then add soy, chillies and oil.

Marinate lamb for 30 minutes.

Drain excess marinade. **lime and chilli lamb cutlets**

Place cutlets on oiled barbecue grill.

Cook for 4 minutes, rotating once.

Turn over and cook for a further 3–4 minutes, rotating once.

≡ Sizzling time 7–8 minutes

Serves 4

8 lamb steaks

3 tbsp olive oil

2 tbsp lemon juice

3 tsp ground cumin

4 tsp toasted cumin seeds

4 tsp caster sugar

1 tsp salt

3 tsp harissa*

Place lamb steaks in dish.

Mix remaining ingredients together.

Marinate lamb for 30 minutes. **lamb with cumin crust**

Place lamb on oiled barbecue grill.

Cook for 3 minutes, rotating once.

Turn over; cook for a further 3 minutes, rotating once.

Serve lamb with babaganoush (page 24).

≡ Sizzling time 6 minutes

Serves 4

indian tikka lamb

Mix tikka paste, lemon juice and yoghurt together.

Dice lamb into 2 cm (³/₄ in) chunks.

Marinate lamb for 30 minutes.

Thread lamb onto skewers.

Place skewers on oiled barbecue hotplate.

Cook for 8 minutes, turning 3–4 times.

Sizzling time 8 minutes

Serves 4

3 tbsp tikka curry paste

2 tbsp lemon juice

100 g (3¹/₂ oz) natural yoghurt

500 g (1 lb) lamb loin

12 skewers

harissa lamb

Mix harissa, spices, lemon juice, oil and mint together.

Marinate lamb for 30 minutes.

Place on oiled barbecue grill and cook for 4 minutes, rotating once.

Turn over and cook for a further 4 minutes, rotating once.

Rest for 5 minutes, then slice.

Serve with Moroccan couscous salad (page 137).

Sizzling time 8 minutes

Serves 4

3 tsp harissa*

1 tsp ground cumin

1 tsp ground coriander

1 tbsp lemon juice

1 tbsp olive oil

2 tbsp chopped mint leaves

4 lamb loins

lamb with mustard and herb crust

Mix mustard, sugar, garlic, herbs and oil together.

Rub over lamb.

Place lamb on oiled barbecue hotplate.

Cook for 4 minutes, rotating once.

Turn over and cook for a further 4 minutes, rotating once.

Rest for 5 minutes.

Slice and serve with potato wedges (page 125).

Sizzling time 8 minutes

Serves 4

50 g (1³/₄ oz) wholegrain mustard

3 tsp soft brown sugar

2 garlic cloves, crushed

2 tbsp chopped coriander leaves

1 tbsp chopped mint

1 tbsp olive oil

4 lamb loins

4 lamb loins

10 cm (4 in) fresh ginger, peeled and chopped

30 g (1 oz) coriander leaves

2 tsp toasted cumin seeds

2 garlic cloves, peeled

2 tbsp lemon juice

2 tsp paprika

1 tsp ground turmeric

1 tsp salt

100 ml (3½ fl oz) olive oil

Place lamb in a bowl.

Place remaining ingredients in the food processor.

Blend until smooth. **ginger-spice lamb**

Marinate lamb for 30 minutes.

Place lamb on oiled barbecue hotplate.

Cook for 4 minutes, rotating once.

Turn over; cook for a further 3–4 minutes, rotating once.

Rest for 5 minutes.

Slice thickly to serve.

■ Sizzling time 7–8 minutes

Serves 4

75 ml (2½ fl oz) olive oil

80 ml (2¾ fl oz) lemon juice

3 garlic cloves, crushed

A handful chopped basil, oregano and parsley

Salt and freshly ground black pepper

1 leg of lamb, boned and laid flat

Mix together oil, lemon juice, garlic, herbs, salt and pepper.

Marinate lamb for 1 hour.

Prepare dressing by putting garlic, lemon juice, parsley and basil in a food processor.

Blend until smooth. **greek leg of lamb**

Gradually add oil, then season to taste.

Place lamb on oiled barbecue hotplate.

Cook for 10 minutes, rotating once.

Reduce heat to low and turn lamb over.

Cover and cook for 10 minutes.

Remove cover, rotate and cook for a further 10 minutes.

Rest for 10 minutes.

Cut into thick slices.

Pour dressing over lamb.

Serve with Greek salad (page 128).

■ Sizzling time 30 minutes

Serves 6

DRESSING

2 garlic cloves, peeled

80 ml (2¾ fl oz) lemon juice

30 g (1 oz) parsley leaves

A handful basil leaves

250 ml (8 fl oz) olive oil

Salt and freshly ground black pepper

Place oregano in a food processor with garlic, salt and pepper.

Process briefly, add oil to moisten and blend until smooth.

oregano lamb with spiced onions   Marinate lamb for 1 hour.

Toss onions with spices, salt, pepper, garlic and oil.

Place onions on oiled barbecue hotplate.

Reduce heat to low and cook for 30 minutes, turning often.

Add extra oil as required.

Place lamb on oiled barbecue grill.

Cook for 3 minutes on each side.

Place onions on platter and arrange lamb slices on top.

Serve with tzaziki (page 142).

Sizzling time 30 minutes ■ ≡

Serves 4

A handful oregano leaves

1 garlic clove

Salt and freshly ground black pepper

3 tbsp olive oil

12 lamb steaks

500 g (1 lb) onions, thinly sliced

2 tbsp ground coriander

1 tbsp ground cumin

⅓ tsp salt

⅓ tsp ground black pepper

1 garlic clove, crushed

75 ml (2½ fl oz) olive oil

Place lamb, onion, ground spices, oregano, harissa and salt in a large bowl.

lamb kofta skewers   Knead well by hand for five minutes.

Refrigerate for 1 hour so flavours can develop.

Soak bulgar wheat in plenty of cold water for 20 minutes. Drain well.

Divide kofta mixture into 12 equal pieces and shape into thick fingers.

Scatter bulgar wheat onto a plate and roll lamb until coated.

Thread skewers through the centre of each kofta.

Place on oiled barbecue grill.

Cook for 12–15 minutes, turning frequently.

Serve with tzaziki (page 142), green salad (page 128) and pitta bread.

Sizzling time 12–15 minutes ≡

Makes 12

This mixture can also be made into burgers and served

in toasted pittas.

1 kg (2 lb) finely ground lamb mince

1 onion, very finely chopped

3 tsp ground coriander

4 tsp ground cumin

½ tsp ground cinnamon

½ tsp ground allspice

½ tsp ground white pepper

2 tsp oregano leaves, chopped

2 tsp harissa*

1 tsp salt

100 g (3½ oz) bulgar wheat*

12 skewers

SPIT-ROASTED LAMB

A spit-roast is a fantastic way to cook for a large group. It will take around two hours to prepare the coals and secure the lamb for roasting.

Your spit-roast should come with instructions on securing the lamb to the main rod. This rod is passed through the lamb lengthways and attached through the centre with long bolts. The legs are then attached to the rod with triangular attachments and these are bolted on tightly. These attachments and bolts will need to be adjusted later as the lamb shrinks during cooking.

The spit should also come with a small motor to turn the lamb during cooking.

YOU WILL NEED:

Charcoal;
Firelighters;
Long matches;
Long-handled shovel; and
Water spray bottle.

LIGHTING UP

Set about 12 firelighters in the bottom of the charcoal tray and surround each with a layer of charcoal.

Light firelighters and mound more charcoal around top as they catch alight. Fan the fires well to ensure they catch.

You'll need quite a hot fire to get the charcoal to a good glowing temperature.

Add a second layer of charcoal and ensure it heats to glowing by fanning.

Be warned, this is a hot job and by the time you're finished you'll smell like charcoal.

Use a long-handled shovel to move the coals around as needed.

More heat is needed at the ends of the spit where the legs are and the lamb is thicker.

1 whole lamb, approx 15 kg (30 lb)

35 sprigs of rosemary

1 whole garlic head, peeled and

thick cloves sliced

FOR BASTING

6 garlic cloves, crushed

150 ml (5 fl oz) lemon juice (6 lemons)

60 g (2 oz) chopped herbs – parsley, basil,

rosemary, thyme and oregano

4 tsp salt

4 tsp freshly ground black pepper

250 ml (8 fl oz) olive oil

kitchen foil

When lamb is on its rod, make deep slits all over (shoulder and legs in particular).

Push rosemary and garlic slices deep into the slits

(if not in deep enough they will come out during cooking).

Place the lamb over the glowing coals and connect the motor to begin turning lamb.

Mix together garlic, lemon juice, herbs, salt, pepper and olive oil.

spit-roasted lamb   Brush lamb all over with this marinade.

During the first 30 minutes of cooking ensure the coals are kept

glowing by fanning where needed.

After 30 minutes some fat will begin to drip from the lamb

onto the fire and create flare-ups.

It is here that the water bottle is essential.

As flare-ups occur, spray well to reduce the flames back to

glowing coals as they will burn rather than cook the meat.

These flare-ups will continue for 30–40 minutes and will require your full attention.

Continue to cook for a further 1½ hours.

To test if lamb is done, insert a knife into the thickest part.

If clear juices appear, the meat is ready.

Rest for at least 20 minutes before carving.

Wrap in kitchen foil if it is a cool or windy day.

Remove the entire lamb to a large table, or carve directly from the spit.

Sizzling time 2½–3 hours

Serves 30–40

pork

Satay pork sugar cane sticks

[pork]

Cuts such as pork ribs and chops cook beautifully on a barbecue, their natural fat melting during cooking, keeping the meat moist. Gutsy flavours such as soy, chilli and spices provide real character to the meat.

To purchase great pork, try to find a good traditional butcher who will have lean, flavoursome meat. Try not to overcook pork. As everyone knows pork should be cooked through, most people overcook it to make sure. Undercooked pork is pink inside, overcooked pork is grey-beige, but perfectly cooked pork should be pearly white in colour and still succulent and juicy.

Pork is also one of the main meats used in the making of sausages, the darling of all barbecues. Most people believe you can't go wrong with sausages, but please make sure they're top quality and cooked right through.

Pork sizzling times

8 minutes	Cutlets
9–10 minutes	Chops
10–15 minutes	Ribs
15 minutes	Fillet
50–60 minutes	Pork neck

Mix soy, honey and five-spice together.

Marinate pork for 2 hours.

simple pork spare ribs   Drain excess marinade.

Use remaining marinade for basting during cooking.

Place pork on medium-heat oiled barbecue grill.

Cook for 10–15 minutes, turning 4–5 times.

Sizzling time 10–15 minutes ≡

Serves 4

250 ml (8 fl oz) soy sauce

2$\frac{1}{2}$ tbsp runny honey

$\frac{1}{2}$ tsp five-spice powder

1 kg (2 lb) pork ribs

Place pork in a bowl.

Put remaining ingredients in a saucepan and bring to the boil.

bbq pork ribs   Reduce to a simmer and cook for 15 minutes.

Adjust seasoning and consistency of basting sauce if required.

Place pork on medium–heat oiled barbecue grill.

Brush regularly with basting sauce.

Cook for 10–15 minutes, turning 4–5 times.

Sizzling time 10–15 minutes ≡

Serves 4

If you want your ribs with a bit more zing, use the marinade from

sweet sticky pork (page 103), or add 2 tsp chilli paste to the recipe above.

1 kg (2 lb) pork ribs

2 tbsp tomato ketchup

1 tbsp Worcestershire sauce

1 tbsp white vinegar

4 tsp brown sugar

2 tsp Dijon mustard

1 tsp chilli powder

Dash of Tabasco

Mix pork mince with peanut butter, ginger and lime zest.

Divide into 10 pieces and shape into balls.

Push one piece of sugar cane through each ball.

satay pork sugar cane sticks   Place pork on oiled barbecue grill.

Cook for 8 minutes, turning 3–4 times.

Serve with hot satay sauce (page 143).

Sizzling time 8 minutes ≡

Makes 10

500 g (1 lb) pork mince

75 g (2$\frac{2}{3}$ oz) crunchy peanut butter

3 tsp grated ginger

Grated zest of 2 limes

10 pieces peeled sugar cane*,

$\frac{1}{2}$ cm x 5 cm ($\frac{1}{4}$ in x 2 in) length,

or 10 skewers

Dice pork into 2 cm (³⁄₄ in) chunks.

Mash black beans with a fork.

500 g (1 lb) pork fillet

Add oil, soy and ginger.

2 tsp black beans*, soaked and drained

Marinate pork for 1 hour.   **chinese pork kebabs with**

2 tsp sesame oil

Drain excess marinade.   **black bean and sesame**

2¹⁄₂ tbsp soy sauce

Thread pork onto skewers.

2 tsp grated ginger

Place pork on oiled barbecue grill.

10 skewers

Cook for 6–8 minutes, turning often.

≡ Sizzling time 6–8 minutes

Makes 10 skewers

Remove excess fat from pork.

Cut into 10 cm x 2 cm (4 in x ³⁄₄ in) pieces.

1 kg (2 lb) belly pork

Place pork in a bowl.   **belly pork with**

2¹⁄₂ tbsp maple syrup

Mix remaining ingredients together.   **maple syrup glaze**

¹⁄₂ tsp ground cinnamon

Marinate pork for 1 hour.

2¹⁄₂ tbsp tomato ketchup

Drain excess marinade.

1 tsp Worcestershire sauce

Use remaining marinade for basting during cooking.

2 tbsp olive oil

Place pork on oiled barbecue grill.

Cook for 15–20 minutes, turning 3–4 times.

≡ Sizzling time 15–20 minutes

Serves 4

Satay pork sugar cane sticks

Sichuan pepper and honey pork fillet

500 g (1 lb) pork mince

Mix all ingredients together until well combined.

6 shiitake mushrooms*, chopped

Divide pork mix into 16 portions.

100 g (3¹/₂ oz) water chestnuts*, chopped

lion's head burgers Form into burger shapes.

1 egg white

Place on oiled barbecue grill; cook for 5–6 minutes, rotating once.

4 spring onions, thinly sliced

Turn over; cook for a further 5–6 minutes, rotating once.

2 tsp grated ginger

3 tsp cornflour

Sizzling time 10–12 minutes ≡

1 tbsp rice wine*

Makes 16

¹/₂ tsp salt

Mix oil, soy and ginger together.

Marinate pork for 1 hour.

2 tsp sesame oil

sesame pork cutlets Drain excess marinade.

2¹/₂ tbsp soy sauce

Sprinkle pork with sesame seeds.

1 tsp grated ginger

Place on oiled barbecue hotplate; cook for 4 minutes, rotating once.

8 pork cutlets

Turn over and cook for a further 4 minutes, rotating once.

50 g (1³/₄ oz) sesame seeds

Sizzling time 8 minutes ■

Serves 4

6 pork loin chops

2 cm (¾ in) ginger, sliced

1 lemongrass stem, sliced

2 kaffir lime leaves*, sliced

1 lime, sliced

1 garlic clove, sliced

125 ml (4 fl oz) coconut milk

125 ml (4 fl oz) water

1 tsp Thai fish sauce

2 tsp brown sugar

Place pork in a bowl.

Combine remaining ingredients in a saucepan.

Bring to a gentle simmer. **pork chops with spiced coconut glaze**

Cook over a low heat for 20–30 minutes, until thickened.

Strain the sauce into a bowl; press down well to extract all flavours.

Baste pork with coconut glaze.

Place chops on oiled barbecue grill.

Cook for 5 minutes, rotating once.

Continue to baste with coconut glaze.

Turn over; cook for a further 4 minutes, rotating once.

≡ Sizzling time 9 minutes

Serves 6

3½ tbsp olive oil

½ tsp ground cinnamon

½ tsp ground ginger

Salt and freshly ground black pepper

4 pork chops

2 apples, peeled, cored and thickly sliced

Combine 2 tablespoons of oil with spices, salt and pepper.

Brush over pork. **pork chops with apples**

Mix apples with remaining olive oil.

Place apples on oiled barbecue hotplate.

Cook for 8 minutes, turning often.

Place pork on oiled barbecue grill.

Cook for 5 minutes, rotating once.

Turn over and cook for a further 4 minutes, rotating once.

Place pork on cooked apples to serve.

■≡ Sizzling time 9 minutes

Serves 4

Toast Sichuan pepper in a small pan until fragrant.

Crush in a mortar and pestle, or food processor.

Mix with oil, five-spice, chilli sauce, honey and salt.

sichuan pepper and honey pork fillet Marinate pork for 1 hour.

Place pork on medium–heat oiled barbecue grill.

Cook for 15 minutes, turning 2–3 times.

Rest for 5 minutes.

Slice and serve.

Sizzling time 15 minutes ≡

Serves 4

1 tsp Sichuan pepper*

2 tsp sesame oil

1 tsp five-spice powder

½ tsp chilli sauce

2 tbsp honey

Pinch of salt

750 g (1½ lb) pork fillet

Place pork neck in a large bowl.

Combine remaining ingredients.

Marinate pork for 2 hours, turning occasionally.

sweet sticky pork Drain excess marinade.

Use remaining marinade for basting during cooking.

Place pork on medium-heat oiled barbecue grill and cook for 10 minutes.

Rotate and cover, cook for 20 minutes.

Turn pork over and cook for 10 minutes.

Rotate, cover and cook for a further 15 minutes.

Check to see if pork is cooked.

Rest for 10 minutes before carving.

Serve with Asian noodle salad (page 133).

Sizzling time 55 minutes ≡

Serves 6

1–1.5 kg (2–3 lb) pork neck

STICKY PORK MARINADE

250 ml (8 fl oz) dark soy sauce

125 ml (4 fl oz) rice vinegar

2 tbsp honey

1 tsp sesame oil

2 garlic cloves, crushed

2 tsp grated ginger

2 tbsp bean paste*

½ tsp five-spice powder

sausages

[sausages]

You will find no complicated sausage recipes here.
No recipes that force you to stick lamb intestines over your
bathroom taps to clean them, then attempt to shove
fancy fillings firmly down the middle. Simply put, we believe
you can buy good sausages much more easily
than you can make them yourself.

However, you should choose good quality sausages
for preference, forget about the special offers at your
local market, or 'barbecue packs' from dubious butchers.
Head instead to a traditional butcher or specialist sausage
shop and savour their range. Many butchers also make
bangers with 'modern' fillings such as lamb, venison,
cheese and leek, or satay pork.

The exception to the sausage-making rule is cevapcici,
a skinless sausage that's incredibly easy to make.

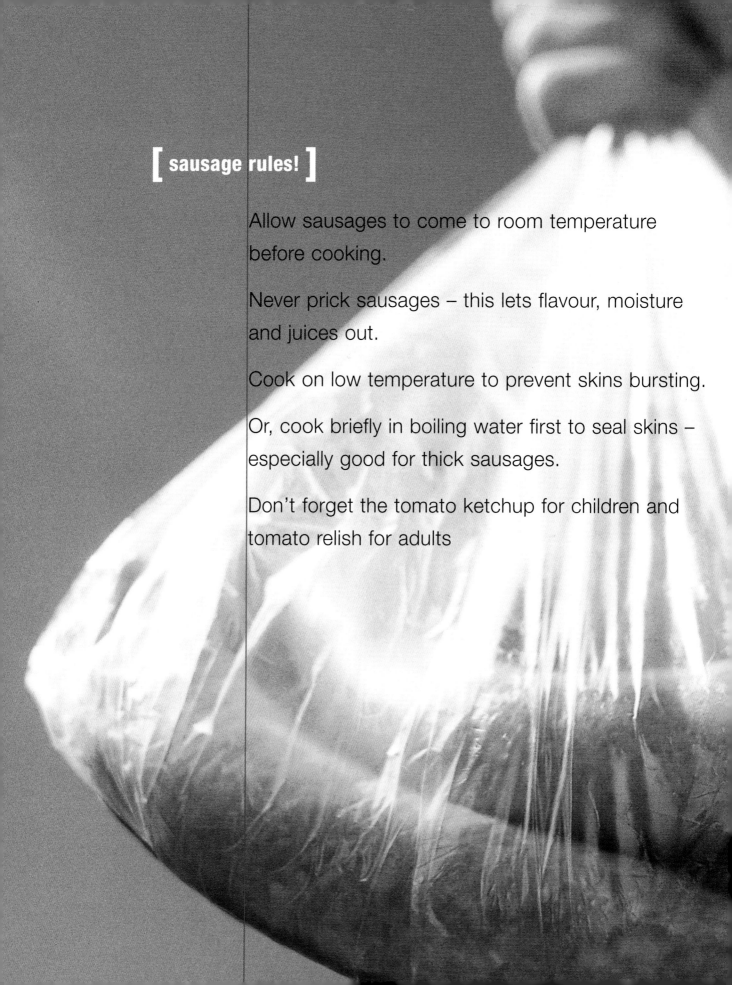

[sausage rules!]

Allow sausages to come to room temperature before cooking.

Never prick sausages – this lets flavour, moisture and juices out.

Cook on low temperature to prevent skins bursting.

Or, cook briefly in boiling water first to seal skins – especially good for thick sausages.

Don't forget the tomato ketchup for children and tomato relish for adults

Put beef, pork and back fat through a course mincer.

Add remaining ingredients and pass through a fine mincer.

Divide mix into 20 x 50 g (1¾ oz) portions.

jonathan's cevapcici

Form into flattened oblong shapes.

Place cevapcici on oiled barbecue grill.

Cook for 6–8 minutes, turning 3–4 times.

Serve with spicy tomato chutney (page 144).

Sizzling time 6–8 minutes

Makes 20

Add 1 tsp chilli powder for a spice hit.

850 g (1¾ lb) beef (topside) and pork (leg)

150 g (5 oz) pork back fat

15 g (½ oz) sea salt flakes

⅓ tsp ground white pepper

Freshly ground black pepper

1 garlic clove, crushed

⅓ tsp nutmeg

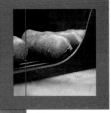

vegetarian

[vegetarian]

Vegetarian food is often overlooked when barbecuing, but this shouldn't be so, as many people now seek and enjoy vegetarian dishes.

A simple plate of barbecued vegetables will keep most people happy, or you could turn those vegetables into kebabs, add some tofu and marinate in pesto for a real flavour hit. Vegetable burgers are another great staple and recipes here include a caramelised onion and chickpea version, plus a lentil and ricotta creation. Risotto can evolve into mushroom cakes by adding egg and breadcrumbs, which are delicious in their own right, or perfect as a side dish to barbecued meats.

Remember, if you are cooking for vegetarians ensure this food is cooked separately from meat, fish and seafood, otherwise you're missing the point of vegetarian food entirely.

250 g (8 oz) firm tofu

1½ tbsp shoyu*

1 tbsp mirin*

1 tsp sesame oil

1 tsp chilli paste

10 skewers

Cut tofu into 1 cm (½ in) chunks and place in a bowl.

Mix remaining ingredients together.

Marinate tofu for 4 hours.

Thread tofu on skewers. **tofu spicy kebabs**

Place on oiled barbecue hotplate.

Cook for 8 minutes, turning 3–4 times.

■ Sizzling time 8 minutes

Makes 10 skewers

250 g (8 oz) firm tofu

2 courgettes, cut into ½ cm (¼ in) slices

20 button mushrooms

3 tsp pesto

1 tbsp red wine vinegar

1 tsp Dijon mustard

1 tbsp olive oil

Salt and freshly ground black pepper

12 skewers

Cut tofu into 2 cm (¾ in) chunks.

Place in a bowl with courgettes and mushrooms.

Mix pesto, vinegar, mustard, oil, salt and pepper together.

Marinate tofu and vegetables for 4 hours. **pesto and tofu**

Thread tofu and vegetables onto skewers. **vegetables sticks**

Place on oiled barbecue hotplate.

Cook for 12 minutes, turning 3–4 times.

■ Sizzling time 12 minutes

Makes 12 skewers

250 g (8 oz) chickpeas,

soaked in cold water overnight

75 ml (2$^1/_2$ fl oz) olive oil

Cook chickpeas in boiling water until soft, approx 30–40 minutes.

4 onions, sliced

Drain and mash roughly.

2 tsp ground cumin

Heat oil in saucepan, add onions, cumin, coriander, paprika and chilli.

2 tsp ground coriander

Cook for 20 minutes on low heat, stirring often until onions soften.

1 tsp paprika

Add spinach and cook until soft.

$^1/_2$ tsp chilli powder

Mix onion/spinach with chickpeas.

150 g (5 oz) spinach leaves, chopped

caramelised onion

Add egg, breadcrumbs and coriander.

1 egg

and chickpea burgers

Mix to combine and season to taste.

100–150 g (3$^1/_2$–5 oz) breadcrumbs

Divide into 12 and form into burger shapes.

A handful coriander leaves

Place burgers on oiled barbecue hotplate.

Salt and freshly ground black pepper

Cook for 6 minutes, rotating once.

Turn over and cook for a further 6 minutes, rotating once.

Sizzling time 12 minutes

Makes 12

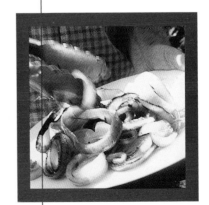

1 tbsp olive oil

1 onion, diced

1 tsp curry paste

200 g (7 oz) red lentils, washed

500 ml (16 fl oz) vegetable stock

2 tbsp chopped fresh herbs

125 g (4 oz) ricotta

100 g (3½ oz) breadcrumbs

Heat a medium-sized saucepan.

Add oil and onion and cook until soft.

Add curry paste and cook for 3–4 minutes.

Add lentils, stir well, and add enough stock to cover.

Bring to the boil, reduce heat. **lentil and ricotta burgers**

Cook for 15 minutes, adding more stock if necessary.

Cook until lentils are tender and all liquid is absorbed.

Place lentils in a bowl, add herbs, ricotta and breadcrumbs.

Mix well and season to taste.

Divide into 12 and form into burger shapes.

Place burgers on oiled barbecue hotplate.

Cook for 5–6 minutes, rotating once.

Turn over; cook for a further 5 minutes, rotating once.

■ Sizzling time 10–11 minutes

Makes 12

Serve with beetroot relish (page 146).

Boil potatoes until tender.

Drain well, mash and stir in butter.

Cook diced vegetables in a pan with olive oil until tender.

Stir vegetables into potato then add herbs.

vegetable burgers   Season to taste.

Divide into 10 and form into burger shapes.

Place burgers on oiled barbecue hotplate.

Cook for 5–6 minutes, rotating once.

Turn over; cook for a further 5 minutes, rotating once.

Serve with roast red pepper relish (page 144).

Sizzling time 10–11 minutes

Makes 10

750 g (1¹/₂ lb) waxy potatoes

25 g (³/₄ oz) butter

1 onion, finely diced

¹/₂ red pepper, finely diced

1 small carrot, finely diced

1 small courgette, finely diced

2¹/₂ tbsp olive oil

3 tbsp chopped fresh herbs

Salt and freshly ground black pepper

Mash tofu roughly with a fork.

Stir in cashew nuts, spring onions, mashed sweet potato and curry paste.

Add salt and pepper to taste.

tofu and cashew nut burgers   Add breadcrumbs.

Divide into 8 and form into burger shapes.

Place burgers on oiled barbecue hotplate and cook for 6 minutes, rotating once.

Turn over; cook for a further 6 minutes, rotating once.

Sizzling time 12 minutes

Makes 8

200 g (7 oz) soft tofu

100 g (3¹/₂ oz) roasted cashew nuts

2 spring onions, thinly sliced

200 g (7 oz) sweet potatoes, boiled and mashed

1 tsp curry paste

Salt and freshly ground black pepper

50 g (1³/₄ oz) breadcrumbs

2 garlic cloves, crushed

$\frac{1}{2}$ tsp ground turmeric

$\frac{1}{2}$ tsp ground cardamom

1 tsp ground coriander

1 tsp ground cumin

2 tbsp chopped coriander leaves

2 tsp caster sugar

Salt and freshly ground black pepper

3 tbsp olive oil

1 aubergine, cut into 2 cm ($\frac{3}{4}$ in) chunks,

salted and rinsed

1 red pepper, cut into 2 cm ($\frac{3}{4}$ in) chunks

1 red onion, cut into wedges

10 skewers

Mix together garlic, spices, coriander leaves, sugar, salt, pepper and oil.

Marinate aubergine, red pepper and onion for 1 hour.

Thread marinated vegetables onto skewers. **vegetable kebabs**

Place kebabs on a medium–heat oiled barbecue grill.

Cook for 15–20 minutes, turning 3–4 times.

Sizzling time 15–20 minutes

Makes 10

75 g ($2\frac{1}{3}$ oz) self-raising flour

150 g (5 oz) polenta

$\frac{1}{2}$ tsp salt

$\frac{1}{2}$ tsp baking powder

1 egg

250 ml (8 fl oz) buttermilk

2 corn cobs

Mix flour, polenta, salt and baking powder together.

Whisk egg and buttermilk together.

Stir wet and dry ingredients until combined and smooth.

Allow to stand for 30 minutes. **polenta corn cakes**

Remove kernels from corn cobs with a sharp knife and stir into mixture.

Place spoonfuls of mixture on oiled barbecue hotplate.

Cook for 3–4 minutes on each side.

Sizzling time 6–8 minutes

Makes 10

Serve for breakfast with barbecued mushrooms and tomatoes,

or make smaller fritters and serve as a pre-dinner nibble

with horseradish cream on top.

Heat a large saucepan over a medium heat.

Add oil, onion, carrot and garlic, cook for 2 minutes, stirring regularly.

Add mushrooms and cook for 3–4 minutes.

Add rice and cook for 1 minute, stirring well.

Add stock to saucepan and simmer until liquid is absorbed, approx 12 minutes.

Allow to cool slightly, stir in Parmesan, basil, egg and breadcrumbs.

mushroom risotto cakes   Season to taste.

Divide into 12 and pat into flat round cakes.

Sprinkle each cake with extra breadcrumbs.

Place risotto cakes on oiled barbecue hotplate.

Cook for 5–6 minutes, rotating once.

Turn over; cook for a further 5 minutes, rotating once.

Sizzling time 10–12 minutes ■

Makes 12

Use any leftover vegetarian risotto to make these cakes.

Add other vegetables such as roasted aubergine, asparagus or pumpkin.

1 tbsp olive oil

1 onion, finely diced

½ small carrot, finely diced

1 garlic clove, crushed

100 g (3½ oz) button mushrooms,

thinly sliced

200 g (7 oz) arborio rice*

800 ml (1½ pt) hot vegetable stock

50 g (1¾ oz) grated Parmesan cheese*

15 basil leaves, thinly sliced

1 egg

25 g (¾ oz) dry breadcrumbs

Salt and freshly ground black pepper

Extra dry breadcrumbs

barbecued polenta and garlic vegetables

POLENTA

500 ml (16 fl oz) water

500 ml (16 fl oz) vegetable stock

180 g (6 oz) polenta

50 g (1¾ oz) grated Parmesan cheese*

Salt to taste

Bring water and stock to the boil in a heavy-based saucepan.

Sprinkle in polenta and stir until mixture returns to the boil.

Reduce heat to low and cook for 20 minutes, stirring often.

Remove from heat, stir through cheese.

Add salt to taste.

Pour into a deep baking dish and allow to set, at least 4 hours.

When set, cut into wedges or triangles.

GARLIC VEGETABLES

2½ tbsp olive oil

3 garlic cloves, crushed

Salt and freshly ground black pepper

2 courgettes, cut in half lengthways

1 small aubergine, cut into 8 wedges, salted

8 mushrooms

2 tomatoes, cut in half

Pesto, optional

Mix oil, garlic, salt and pepper together.

Place vegetables and polenta on oiled barbecue grill.

Baste vegetables with garlic oil during cooking.

Cook for 10 minutes, turning 2–3 times.

Serve vegetables on top of polenta with a dollop of pesto.

≡ Sizzling time 10 minutes

Serves 4

Polenta corn cakes

Place aubergine on oiled barbecue hotplate.

Cook until tender and golden brown on each side, 5–6 minutes.

goat's cheese and aubergine sandwiches Add more oil as necessary.

Place goat's cheese, rocket and basil between 2 pieces of cooked aubergine.

Grind black pepper over the top and serve while still warm.

Sizzling time 5–6 minutes ■

Makes 8

2 medium aubergines, cut into 1 cm (¹/₂ in) slices,

salted and rinsed

Olive oil

200 g (7 oz) firm goat's cheese

100 g (3¹/₂ oz) rocket leaves, washed

Fresh basil leaves

Freshly ground black pepper

vegetables

[vegetables]

Whether your tastes run to sweet paprika corn cobs
or you simply want tasty potato wedges, the barbecue is
a great way to go. Bearing in mind that the meat or fish
you are eating is probably in a spicy marinade, it pays
to keep the vegetables simple; perhaps tomatoes with
basil butter, barbecued onion rings or asparagus with feta.

Some vegetables could have been created especially
for the barbecue; just think of aubergines, courgettes or even
radicchio cooked on the barbecue grill. Mushrooms are a
wonderful addition to any meal, especially when brushed
with garlic butter as they cook.

If you are using a wood-fired barbecue make the most
of the coals and roast potatoes and onions in foil.
You are limited only by your imagination.

asparagus with feta

500 g (1 lb) asparagus spears

Olive oil

Salt and freshly ground black pepper

100 g (3½ oz) feta cheese

Trim asparagus spears of woody ends.

Toss with oil, salt and pepper.

Place asparagus on oiled barbecue grill.

Cook for 3–4 minutes, turning 2–3 times.

Arrange on a platter.

Crumble feta on top and serve.

≡ Sizzling time 3–4 minutes

Serves 4–6

Try substituting feta cheese with shaved Parmesan.

tomatoes with basil butter

100 g (3½ oz) soft butter

2 tbsp chopped basil leaves

Freshly ground black pepper

6 tomatoes, cut in half

Olive oil for cooking

Mix butter, basil and pepper together.

Brush tomato halves with olive oil.

Place tomatoes on oiled barbecue grill.

Cook for 6–8 minutes, turning once.

Place on a platter and top each tomato with a little basil butter.

≡ Sizzling time 6–8 minutes

Makes 12

Try this recipe with bacon for breakfast.

barbecued onion rings

1 kg (2 lb) red onions, sliced into 1 cm (½ in) rings

2 tbsp olive oil

Sprigs of fresh thyme

Salt and freshly ground black pepper

Toss onions with oil, thyme, salt and pepper.

Place onions on barbecue hotplate, spread out over the entire surface.

Reduce heat to low and cook for 30 minutes, turning often.

Add extra oil as required.

The onion rings will come apart a little as they are turned.

Remove herb stalks before serving.

■ Sizzling time 30 minutes

Serves 6–8

1 kg (2 lb) onions, thinly sliced

2 tbsp olive oil

Place the onions in a bowl with all the other ingredients.

caramelised onions Mix together well.

1 tbsp sherry vinegar

2 tsp brown sugar

Place onions on oiled barbecue hotplate, spread out over the entire surface.

2 tsp crushed garlic

Reduce heat to low and cook for 30 minutes, turning often.

4 sprigs fresh thyme

Add extra oil as required.

½ tsp salt

Remove herb stalks before serving.

⅓ tsp freshly ground black pepper

Sizzling time 30 minutes ■

Serves 6–8

Brush radicchio wedges with olive oil.

Place on a medium-heat oiled barbecue grill.

2 radicchio heads, outside leaves removed,

cut into 8 wedges

radicchio Cook for 10–12 minutes, turning regularly.

Olive oil

with gorgonzola Dot with small pieces of gorgonzola.

150 g (5 oz) gorgonzola cheese

Sizzling time 10–12 minutes ≡

Makes 16

Wipe mushrooms with a damp cloth.

garlic mushrooms Mix oil with garlic, salt and pepper.

Place mushrooms on barbecue hotplate, brush with garlic oil.

Cook for 4 minutes, brushing with oil, rotating once.

Turn over and brush with garlic oil.

12 chestnut or field mushrooms

Cook for a further 4 minutes, rotating once.

100 ml (3½ fl oz) olive oil

Sizzling time 8 minutes ■

2 garlic cloves, crushed

Serves 4–6

Salt and freshly ground black pepper

150 g (5 oz) chestnut or field mushrooms

150 g (5 oz) oyster mushrooms

100 g (3½ oz) button mushrooms

100 ml (3½ fl oz) olive oil

A handful chopped fresh herbs

Salt and freshly ground black pepper

Wipe mushrooms with a damp cloth.

Mix oil, herbs, salt and pepper together.

Toss oil and mushrooms together. **mushrooms with fresh herbs**

Place mushrooms on oiled barbecue hotplate.

Cook for 15 minutes, turning often.

Add extra oil as required.

■ Sizzling time 15 minutes

Serves 4–6

2 medium sweet potatoes

2 tbsp sesame oil

Salt and freshly ground black pepper

Cut sweet potatoes in half lengthways.

Then cut each half lengthways into 4 wedges.

Mix oil, salt and pepper together. **sesame sweet potato wedges**

Place wedges on oiled barbecue grill, brush with oil and cook for 4 minutes.

Turn onto side; brush with oil and cook for 3 minutes.

Turn onto last side; brush with oil and cook for 3 minutes.

☰ Sizzling time 10 minutes

Serves 4–6

3 corn cobs

3 tbsp olive oil

2 tsp paprika

Salt

Remove green husks and silky tassels from corn.

Cut each cob into 6 slices. **sweet paprika corn cobs**

Mix oil, paprika and salt together.

Toss corn with seasoned oil.

Place corn slices on oiled barbecue grill.

Cook for 10 minutes, turning often.

☰ Sizzling time 10 minutes

Serves 4

Cut potatoes into thick wedges and place in a bowl.

potato wedges – one   Add oil, salt and pepper, toss well.

Place wedges on oiled barbecue grill.

Cook until golden, turning regularly.

Sizzling time 30 minutes ≡

Serves 4–6

1 kg (2 lb) medium potatoes

2 tbsp olive oil

Salt and freshly ground black pepper

Cook potatoes in boiling water until tender.

potato wedges – two   Drain, cool and cut into thick wedges.

Place in a bowl, add oil, salt and pepper, toss well.

Place wedges on oiled barbecue grill.

Cook until golden, turning regularly.

Sizzling time 10 minutes ≡

Serves 4–6

1 kg (2 lb) medium potatoes

2 tbsp olive oil

Salt and freshly ground black pepper

Peel and grate the potatoes.

potato roesti   Squeeze excess liquid out.

Mix potato with spring onions, salt and pepper.

Spoon small mounds of roesti mix onto oiled barbecue hotplate and flatten slightly.

Cook until golden brown, approx 3–4 minutes on each side.

Sizzling time 6–8 minutes ■

Makes 10

600 g (1 lb 4 oz) waxy potatoes

4 spring onions, green tops only, thinly sliced

Salt and freshly ground black pepper

cool salads

[cool salads]

It's not a barbecue unless there's some salad on offer.
Keeping this in mind, we've included recipes that range from
simple green leaves and the obligatory potato salad,
to the more exotic Asian coleslaw and watercress tabouleh.

Mostly we've taken summer ingredients and combined
them in interesting ways, such as the green bean, almond and
feta salad and a tomato and white bean salad. A bit more of
a challenge is the barbecued vegetable salad, which combines
wedges of aubergine, courgette, pepper and mushrooms
with a basil dressing.

These recipes will make enough to feed 6 to 8 people.
Naturally, the more people you're feeding, the more salads
you'll need to make.

green salad

250 g (8 oz) salad leaves, washed

½ cucumber, peeled and thinly sliced

2 tbsp red wine vinegar

½ tsp Dijon mustard

Salt and freshly ground black pepper

125 ml (4 fl oz) extra virgin olive oil

Toss salad leaves and cucumber together.

Mix vinegar, mustard, salt and pepper together.

Add oil and whisk well.

Drizzle dressing over salad.

Serves 6

Choose your favourite leaves. You may prefer just Cos, or may like to add radicchio for a striking contrast in both taste and appearance.

greek salad

½ cucumber

½ red pepper

200 g (7 oz) feta cheese

3 ripe tomatoes

½ red onion, thinly sliced

1 Cos lettuce, washed

100 g (3½ oz) Kalamata olives

2 tbsp chopped parsley

1½ tbsp lemon juice

Salt and freshly ground black pepper

80 ml (2¾ fl oz) extra virgin olive oil

Peel cucumber and remove seeds. Slice thinly.

Dice red pepper into 1 cm (½ in) squares.

Dice feta the same size.

Cut tomatoes into wedges.

Mix cucumber, red pepper, feta, tomatoes, onion, lettuce, olives and parsley in a bowl.

Whisk lemon juice, salt and pepper together.

Add oil and whisk well.

Drizzle dressing over salad.

Serves 6

Boil potatoes until just cooked.

Drain and allow to cool.

Cut into 1 cm (¹/₂ in) slices.

potato salad Arrange on platter.

Chop capers and scatter over potatoes with cornichons and parsley.

Drizzle mayonnaise over potato slices.

Grind fresh black pepper over to serve.

Serves 6

1.5 kg (3 lb) waxy potatoes, washed

(peeled if preferred)

3 tsp salted capers, soaked, rinsed and drained

10 cornichons*, chopped

3 tbsp chopped flat leaf parsley

Freshly ground black pepper

Combine egg yolks, salt, pepper and mustard together.

mayonnaise Whisk until white and creamy.

Slowly add oil, whisking continuously.

Add lemon juice to taste.

Make by hand for a creamy effect or in the food processor

for a sleeker white mayonnaise. The choice is yours.

2 egg yolks

Salt and freshly ground black pepper

¹/₂ tsp Dijon mustard

100 ml (3¹/₂ fl oz) extra virgin olive oil

1 tbsp lemon juice

100 g (3¹/₂ oz) white beans (cannellini),

soaked overnight

3 ripe tomatoes, diced

1 cucumber, diced

2 spring onions, thinly sliced

1 tbsp chopped mint leaves

2 tbsp lemon juice

2 tbsp olive oil

Salt and freshly ground black pepper

Drain soaked beans and rinse under cold running water.

Cook in boiling water until tender, approx 30 minutes.

Drain and cool. **tomato and white bean salad**

Mix beans with other salad ingredients and season to taste.

Serves 6.

150 g (5 oz) bulgar wheat*

1 bunch watercress or 100 g (3¹/₂ oz)

rocket, washed

¹/₂ red onion, finely diced

500 g (1 lb) firm ripe tomatoes, diced

3 tbsp lemon juice

125 ml (4 fl oz) extra virgin olive oil

Salt and freshly ground black pepper

Soak bulgar wheat in cold water for 20 minutes, drain well.

Chop watercress (or rocket) roughly.

Place bulgar wheat, watercress, onion and tomatoes in a bowl.

Mix well. **watercress tabouleh**

Add lemon juice and olive oil.

Season to taste with salt and pepper.

Serves 6

500 g (1 lb) green beans, trimmed

100 g (3½ oz) flaked almonds, toasted

100 g (3½ oz) feta cheese, crumbled

2 tbsp chopped parsley leaves

1 tbsp red wine vinegar

Salt and freshly ground black pepper

3 tbsp olive oil

Cook beans in boiling water for 2 minutes.

Refresh under cold water immediately.

Cut beans in half and place on a platter.

Top with almonds, feta and parsley. **green bean, almond**

Whisk vinegar, salt and pepper together. **and feta salad**

Add oil and whisk well.

Drizzle dressing over salad.

Serves 6

½ Chinese cabbage, sliced

2 carrots, shredded

6 spring onions, thinly sliced

A handful coriander leaves

20 g (¾ oz) shaved palm sugar*,

or soft brown sugar

2 tbsp Thai fish sauce

3 tbsp lime juice

Freshly ground black pepper

3 tbsp groundnut oil

Toss Chinese cabbage, carrot, spring onions and coriander together.

Dissolve sugar in fish sauce and lime juice.

Add pepper and whisk in oil.

Toss vegetables with dressing.

Serves 6. **asian coleslaw**

To shred carrot for salad, peel long slices from the length

of carrot using a vegetable peeler.

Boil soba noodles in plenty of boiling water for 6–8 minutes.

asian noodle salad Refresh under cold water.

Cook mangetout in boiling water for 2 minutes.

Refresh under cold water and slice thinly.

Toss all ingredients together.

Dissolve sugar in lime juice, fish sauce and mirin.

Add pepper, coriander and oil.

Whisk together well.

To serve, mix salad with dressing.

Serves 6

Substitute soba noodles with cellophane rice noodles if preferred.

125 g (4 oz) soba noodles

100 g (3¹/₂ oz) mangetout

¹/₂ red pepper, finely diced

1 carrot, shredded

1 cucumber, thinly sliced

4 red shallots, thinly sliced

20 mint leaves, shredded

MIRIN DRESSING

25 g (³/₄ oz) shaved palm sugar*,

or soft brown sugar

1¹/₂ tbsp lime juice

1 tbsp Thai fish sauce

2 tbsp mirin*

Freshly ground black pepper

2 tbsp chopped coriander leaves

100 ml (3¹/₂ fl oz) groundnut oil

barbecued vegetable salad

1 aubergine, cut into 8 wedges, salted and rinsed

2 small courgettes, cut lengthways into quarters

1 red pepper, cut in 6 wedges, seeds removed

100 g (3½ oz) small mushrooms

3 tbsp olive oil

1 tbsp sherry vinegar

Salt and freshly ground black pepper

DRESSING

3 tbsp olive oil

1 tbsp sherry vinegar

20 basil leaves, thinly sliced

Toss vegetables with oil, vinegar, salt and pepper.

Place vegetables on oiled barbecue grill.

Cook for 20–30 minutes.

Turn regularly; adding extra oil if needed.

Place vegetables on a platter.

Whisk together oil and vinegar.

Drizzle dressing over vegetables.

Sprinkle basil on top.

Sizzling time 30 minutes

Serves 6–8

simple bok choy salad

150 g (5 oz) baby bok choy*, washed

A handful coriander leaves

½ red pepper, thinly sliced

6 spring onions, thinly sliced

4 red shallots, thinly sliced

1½ tbsp lime juice

1 tsp Thai fish sauce

Salt and freshly ground black pepper

125 ml (4 fl oz) groundnut oil

Toss bok choy, coriander, red pepper, spring onions and shallots together.

Place in a serving bowl.

Whisk lime juice, fish sauce, salt, pepper and oil together.

Pour dressing over salad.

Serves 6

Beetroot relish

Peaches with goat's curd and honey

Heat oil in a saucepan.

Add couscous; stir to coat with oil.

Add water and salt and bring to the boil.

Simmer until all liquid has been absorbed.

Tip couscous into a large bowl and allow to cool.

Mix couscous with remaining ingredients.

moroccan couscous salad Season to taste.

Whisk all dressing ingredients together.

Spoon dressing over the couscous.

Serves 6

3 tbsp olive oil

200 g (7 oz) instant couscous*

250 ml (8 fl oz) water

Pinch of salt

100 g (3½ oz) canned chickpeas

200 g (7 oz) pumpkin, cut into

½ cm (¼ in) dice and roasted

½ red pepper, cut into ½ cm (¼ in) chunks

100 g (3½ oz) toasted pine nuts

A handful chopped coriander leaves

Salt and freshly ground black pepper

YOGURT DRESSING

150 g (5 oz) natural yogurt

2 tsp chopped fresh mint

Freshly ground black pepper

2 tbsp lemon juice

relishes and sauces

[relishes and sauces]

It wouldn't be a barbecue without some kind of sauce.
While the commercial tomato ketchup reigns supreme
at most barbies, it's not hard to do a little better.

Simple salsas made with freshly chopped tomatoes
and herbs are beautiful with any grilled meat. And then,
there's lemon butter sauce, great with grilled fish fillets,
or perhaps green olive salsa with well, just about everything.

Set aside an hour to make the spicy tomato relish and
you'll have enough to last all summer. If you want something
a little more unusual, try the sage and walnut mustard.
You'll be amazed at how easy it is, and how good
it is with steak. Then, of course, there's BBQ sauce
– make your own and add it to everything!

fresh mango salsa

1 ripe mango

1 tsp caster sugar

1 tbsp lime juice

2 tsp Thai fish sauce

2 small red chillies, finely diced

1 tbsp chopped Thai basil* or coriander leaves

Freshly ground black pepper

Peel mango.

Remove flesh from stone and dice finely.

Dissolve sugar in lime juice and fish sauce.

Add remaining ingredients and mix to combine.

Serve with Asian-style dishes.

tomato and fresh herb salsa

4 ripe tomatoes

½ cucumber

6 basil leaves, thinly sliced

A few drops sherry or balsamic vinegar

A few drops olive oil

Salt and freshly ground black pepper

Dice tomatoes finely.

Dice cucumber to the same size.

Mix tomato, cucumber and basil together.

Season to taste with vinegar, olive oil, salt and pepper.

Choose the herb to suit your tastes or the dish;

coriander for Asian-style dishes, mint for Moroccan

and basil or parsley for Mediterranean.

green papaya salsa

1 green papaya

½ red pepper

10 mint leaves

20 g (¾ oz) shaved palm sugar*,

or soft brown sugar

1½ tbsp lime juice

1 tbsp Thai fish sauce

1 tsp grated ginger

Grated zest of 1 lime

1 tbsp groundnut oil

Freshly ground black pepper

Peel papaya and remove seeds.

Dice flesh finely.

Slice red pepper thinly and dice finely.

Thinly slice mint leaves; combine with papaya and red pepper.

Dissolve sugar in lime juice and fish sauce.

Mix together with remaining ingredients.

Stand for 30 minutes before serving.

Serve with shellfish or chicken.

fennel relish

Cut fennel bulb in half.

Discard core and dice fennel finely.

Toss together with lemon juice, salt, pepper and oil.

Serve immediately.

1 fennel bulb

2 tbsp lemon juice

Salt and freshly ground black pepper

2$\frac{1}{2}$ tbsp extra virgin olive oil

Mix together mint, oil, spring onions, sugar and lemon zest.

fresh mint and green onion salsa   Add lemon juice to taste.

Season with salt and pepper.

Serve with shellfish.

A handful mint leaves, thinly sliced

1 tbsp olive oil

3 spring onions, thinly sliced

$\frac{1}{2}$ tsp caster sugar

Grated zest of 2 lemons

4 tbsp lemon juice

Salt and freshly ground black pepper

Finely chop olives, capers and anchovies.

Add parsley, oil and pepper to season.

green olive salsa   Set aside until needed.

Allow to come to room temperature before serving.

Good with fish or chicken.

200 g (7 oz) pitted green olives

2 tsp capers, soaked and rinsed

2 canned anchovy fillets

A handful chopped flat leaf parsley

100 ml (3$\frac{1}{2}$ fl oz) extra virgin olive oil

Freshly ground black pepper

2¹/₂ tbsp white wine

100 g (3¹/₂ oz) soft butter, diced

2 tbsp lemon juice

Salt and freshly ground black pepper

Place white wine in a small saucepan over a medium heat.

Simmer until reduce by half. **lemon butter sauce**

Reduce heat and whisk butter in, piece by piece.

Remove from heat, add lemon juice and season.

Keep warm until ready to serve.

Good with seafood.

To make saffron butter sauce, add a pinch of saffron strands to wine,

then reduce. Omit lemon juice. Add 1 tbsp hot water to thin sauce if necessary.

350 g (12 oz) thick natural yogurt

1 garlic clove, crushed

¹/₂ cucumber, grated

Pinch of dried mint

A small handful coriander, parsley or basil leaves

Pinch of salt

Freshly ground black pepper

Mix all ingredients together.

Season to taste. **tzaziki**

Serve with any spicy food, or use as a dip with Indian bread (page 26).

If your yogurt is a bit thin, place in a dry tea towel in a sieve over a bowl.

Leave to drain in the refrigerator for 4 hours. Discard excess whey.

1 tsp caster sugar

1¹/₂ tbsp lime juice

3 tbsp Thai fish sauce

1 red chilli, finely diced

Dissolve sugar in lime juice.

Add fish sauce and chilli. **thai dipping sauce**

Serve with seafood or chicken.

3 tsp caster sugar

1 tbsp rice vinegar

tamarind dipping sauce

2½ tbsp tamarind water*

Dissolve sugar in vinegar.

2 tsp Thai fish sauce

Add other ingredients.

20 g (¾ oz) finely crushed roasted peanuts

Good with seafood.

70 g (2½ oz) roasted peanuts

30 g (1 oz) coriander leaves

1 large green chilli

Place all ingredients, except oil, in food processor.

coriander pesto Process briefly.

1½ tbsp lime juice

Slowly add oil to form a smooth paste.

1 tbsp Thai fish sauce

1 tsp grated ginger

1 garlic clove

75 ml (2½ fl oz) groundnut oil

1 small onion, diced

1 tbsp soy sauce

Place all ingredients in food processor.

3 tbsp groundnut oil

satay sauce Blend until smooth.

2 tsp ground coriander

Place in a saucepan and bring to the boil.

1 tsp ground cumin

Reduce heat and simmer for 5 minutes.

1 tsp ground turmeric

Serve with beef satay kebabs (page 77).

⅓ tsp cinnamon

1 tsp salt

1 tsp sugar

50 g (1¾ oz) roasted peanuts

200 ml (7 fl oz) coconut milk

5 red peppers

4 tbsp olive oil

2 onions, sliced

2 garlic cloves, crushed

200 g (7 oz) sugar

125 ml (4 fl oz) white wine vinegar

1 tsp ground cinnamon

1 tsp freshly ground black pepper

125 ml (4 fl oz) water

Rub peppers with 2 tablespoons of oil and roast at 200ºC (390ºF/gas mark 6).

Cook for 20–25 minutes until skins blister. **roast red pepper relish**

Place peppers in a plastic bag and seal to allow steam to lift skins.

When cool, remove skins and seeds and dice flesh roughly.

Add remaining olive oil to a large saucepan and cook onion and garlic until soft.

Add red pepper, sugar, vinegar, cinnamon, pepper and water.

Bring to the boil, reduce heat and simmer.

Cook for 30 minutes or until sauce thickens slightly.

Season and spoon into sterilised jars.

Makes 650 ml (1 pt 2 fl oz)

Good with any meat or sausages.

100 ml (3½ fl oz) vegetable oil

2 tsp black mustard seeds

1 tsp grated ginger

3 garlic cloves, crushed

4 tsp chilli paste

1 tsp ground cumin

1 kg (2 lb) ripe tomatoes, chopped

100 ml (3½ fl oz) white wine vinegar

75 g (2⅔ oz) sugar

Salt

Heat oil over a medium heat in a large saucepan.

Add mustard seeds, ginger, garlic, chilli paste and cumin.

Fry for 5–10 minutes, stirring often.

Add tomatoes, cook for 5 minutes.

Add vinegar and sugar. **spicy tomato chutney**

Reduce heat and simmer for 1 hour.

Adjust seasoning if necessary and spoon into sterilised jars.

Makes 750 ml (1¼ pt)

250 g (8 oz) fresh red chillies, such as

cayenne, poblano or serrano

4 garlic cloves, crushed

400 ml (13 fl oz) water

220 g (7¾ oz) caster sugar

4 tsp salt

1 tbsp white wine vinegar

Remove seeds and membrane from chillies and slice thinly.

Place chillies in a saucepan with remaining ingredients.

sweet chilli sauce   Bring to the boil, reduce heat.

Simmer until most of the liquid has evaporated, approx 30 minutes.

Whiz in the blender to produce a thick sauce with flecks of chilli.

Makes 300 ml (½ pt)

Use anywhere you need a sweet, spicy burst.

Bring vinegar, sugar, onion, garlic and ginger to the boil.

mango chutney   Reduce by half.

Add mango and cook for a further 5 minutes.

Remove from the heat and pour into sterilised jars.

Makes 1.25 litres (2 pints)

Good with chicken.

150 ml (5 fl oz) white wine vinegar

100 g (3½ oz) brown sugar

1 onion, finely diced

4 garlic cloves

1 tsp ground ginger

4 mangoes, peeled and sliced

500 g (1 lb) plums, quartered

3 tbsp vinegar

50 g (1¾ oz) brown sugar

2 tbsp grated ginger

125 ml (4 fl oz) water

1 tbsp Indonesian soy sauce*

plum and ginger sauce

Place all ingredients in a saucepan and bring to the boil.

Reduce heat and simmer for 20 minutes, or until plums are cooked.

Strain sauce to remove plum skins.

Makes 500 ml (16 fl oz)

Good with sausages and any game meats.

3 medium beetroots

250 ml (8 fl oz) water

250 ml (8 fl oz) white wine vinegar

75 g (2⅔ oz) brown sugar

2 whole cloves

2 tsp grated ginger

2 garlic cloves

1 small red chilli

12 peppercorns

Cover beetroots with water and cook until tender.

Allow to cool, peel and grate roughly.

Place remaining ingredients in a saucepan and bring to the boil.

Allow to reduce by half. **beetroot relish**

Strain liquid over grated beetroot.

Return to a clean saucepan and simmer for 10 minutes.

Makes 500 ml (16 fl oz)

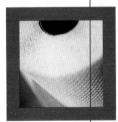

sage and walnut mustard

Place mustard seeds, juice, vinegar and salt in a bowl.

Allow to stand for 48 hours.

Place in a food processor and add walnuts and sage.

Process until combined.

The smoother you make it, the hotter it will be.

Season if required.

Makes 500 ml (16 fl oz)

Serve with beef, veal and game dishes.

100 g (3$\frac{1}{2}$ oz) yellow mustard seeds

250 ml (8 fl oz) grape juice

100 ml (3$\frac{1}{2}$ fl oz) red wine vinegar

2 tsp salt

75 g (2$\frac{2}{3}$ oz) walnuts, roughly chopped

3–4 sprigs fresh sage

bbq sauce

Place all ingredients in a saucepan and bring to the boil.

Reduce to a simmer and cook for 15 minutes.

Adjust seasoning and consistency if required.

Makes 300 ml (½ pt)

Serve with any full-flavoured meat, or use as a marinade.

100 ml (3$\frac{1}{2}$ fl oz) tomato purée or ketchup

2 tbsp Worcestershire sauce

2 tbsp red wine vinegar

100 g (3$\frac{1}{2}$ oz) brown sugar

4 tsp Dijon mustard

2 garlic cloves, crushed

250 ml (8 fl oz) water

summer desserts

You're not going to find too many barbecued rum bananas or tropical pineapple recipes in this chapter. We believe that after sizzling on the barbecue for an afternoon or evening, most people are only too happy to leave it.

The recipes here include classics such as chocolate fudge cake, pavlova with berries and a choice of three tarts: lemon ricotta, passionfruit and frangipane. Other desserts we love to serve at a barbecue are here too, like cooling panne cotta puddings and rosé poached berries with shortbread, both of which can be prepared a day or so beforehand.

If you're really determined to keep the barbecue going, and are prepared to clean it really well, peach halves can be cooked on the grill and served with soft goat's cheese and honey.

Simplest of all, though, is to serve platters of juicy fruit; watermelons, apricots, nectarines, pineapple, cherries and mangoes, sliced and ready to eat.

4 peaches, cut in half and stone removed

100 g (3¹⁄₂ oz) soft goat's cheese

4 tbsp full-flavoured honey

Cook peach halves in a hot oven 200–220°C (390–425°F/gas mark 6–7) or flesh side down on an oiled barbecue grill. **peaches with goat's cheese**

Cook for 5–6 minutes, rotating once. **and honey**

Divide goat's cheese between peaches and drizzle with honey.

≡ Sizzling time 5–6 minutes

Serves 4

2 cardamom pods

375 ml (12³⁄₄ fl oz) milk

375 ml (12³⁄₄ fl oz) cream

75 g (2²⁄₃ oz) caster sugar

2 sheets gelatine*

2 tbsp rosewater*

Almond oil

6 figs

Icing sugar

2 tbsp rosewater*, additional

Crush cardamom pods using a rolling pin.

Heat milk, cream, sugar and cardamom pods gently over a medium heat.

Stir to dissolve sugar and gradually bring to the boil.

Add gelatine to hot milk and whisk until completely dissolved.

Strain hot milk through a sieve to remove cardamom pods.

Add rosewater. **rosewater and cardamom panne cotta with figs**

Brush 6 x 150 ml (5 fl oz) dariole moulds or ramekins lightly with almond oil.

Divide mixture between moulds and refrigerate until set, preferably overnight.

To serve, remove puddings from moulds.

Halve figs and dust with icing sugar.

Cook briefly in a hot oven 200–220°C (390–425°F/gas mark 6–7),

or on an oiled barbecue grill for 2–3 minutes.

Remove, sprinkle with additional rosewater and serve alongside panne cotta.

Serves 6

Rub flour, rice flour, butter, sugar and salt together to form a soft biscuit dough.

Knead for 1 minute on a lightly floured board until well combined.

Roll shortbread to ½ cm (¼ in) thick and cut out large hearts.

Place hearts on a buttered baking tray and bake in preheated oven

170°C (340°F/gas mark 3½) until crisp, approx 10–12 minutes.

Allow to cool on tray for 5 minutes.

Lift gently to a wire rack and allow to cool.

Makes approx 18 large shortbread hearts.

SHORTBREAD

260 g (9 oz) plain flour

115 g (4 oz) rice flour*

250 g (8 oz) butter, diced and softened slightly

110 g (3¾ oz) caster sugar

A pinch of salt

rosé poached berries with shortbread

Place rosé, sugar and lemon juice in a saucepan.

Simmer until reduced by half.

Add strawberries and blackberries and cook for 1 minute.

Add remaining berries, cook for 30 seconds only.

Pour gently into a shallow bowl and chill.

To serve, place two shortbread hearts on each plate.

Top with a pile of berries and syrup.

Serve with clotted cream.

Serves 6

POACHED BERRIES

750 ml (1¼ pt) rosé wine

220 g (7½ oz) caster sugar

2 tbsp lemon juice

250 g (8 oz) strawberries,

stems removed and fruit halved

150 g (5 oz) blackberries, stems removed

150 g (5 oz) raspberries

150 g (5 oz) blueberries

250 ml (8 fl oz) clotted cream

6 egg whites

Beat egg whites until stiff peaks form.

440 g (14 oz) caster sugar

Add caster sugar, one-third at a time, allowing each to be well incorporated.

1 tsp vanilla extract*

Fold through vanilla, cornflour and vinegar. **pavlova with berries**

20 g (³/₄ oz) cornflour

Spoon into a greased 23 cm (9 in) cake tin.

1¹/₂ tsp white vinegar

Place in preheated oven 140°C (280°F/gas mark 1), reduce temperature to

200 ml (7 fl oz) double cream, whipped

120°C (245°F/gas mark ¹/₂) and bake for 45 minutes.

500 g (1 lb) fresh berries

Turn oven off and leave pavlova to cool inside the oven.

Remove pavlova from tin and place on serving platter.

Cover with thick cream, top with berries.

Serves 8

8 red plums

Cut plums in half, remove stones and place in ceramic flan tin.

A handful caster sugar

Sprinkle with sugar. **plum clafouti**

3 eggs

Bake in a preheated oven 190°C (375°F/gas mark 5) for 15–20 minutes until softened.

110 g (3³/₄ oz) caster sugar, additional

Beat eggs, additional sugar, yogurt, milk, flour and vanilla to make a smooth batter.

250 g (8 oz) yogurt

Pour batter over plums and return to the oven.

250 ml (8 fl oz) milk

Bake for 45 minutes, or until puffed and golden.

40 g (1¹/₃ oz) self-raising flour

Serves 6

1 tsp vanilla extract*

chocolate fudge cake

Place butter, chocolate, sugar and coffee in a large saucepan.

Cook over a low heat until melted, stirring often.

Remove from heat.

Add flour, ground almonds, cocoa and eggs and beat well until smooth.

Pour into a greased and lined 23 cm (9 in) cake tin.

Bake in a preheated oven 180ºC (350ºF/gas mark 4) for 45–55 minutes,

or until skewer comes out clean.

Serve with cream.

Serves 8

250 g (8 oz) butter, diced

150 g (5 oz) dark chocolate

250 g (8 oz) caster sugar

250 ml (8 fl oz) strong coffee

150 g (5 oz) self-raising flour

100 g (3¾ oz) ground almonds

50 g (1¾ oz) cocoa

2 eggs

Cream, to serve

raspberry, vanilla and almond slice

Rub together sugar, flour and butter.

Divide mixture in half.

Press half into lined 23 cm (9 in) cake tin and press down firmly.

Bake in a preheated oven 180ºC (350ºF/gas mark 4) for 20 minutes.

Add milk, vanilla and egg to remaining mix.

Scatter baked half with raspberries, then pour over remaining mixture.

Sprinkle almonds on top.

Return to the oven and cook for a further 30 minutes, or until risen and firm to touch.

Slice into wedges to serve.

Serves 8

350 g (12 oz) caster sugar

300 g (10 oz) self-raising flour

125 g (4 oz) soft butter

250 ml (8 fl oz) milk

1 tsp vanilla extract*

1 egg

250 g (8 oz) raspberries

50 g (1¾ oz) flaked almonds

300 g (10 oz) plain flour

Pinch of salt

150 g (5 oz) soft butter

1 egg

50 g (1¾ oz) caster sugar

Place flour, salt and butter in a bowl.

Rub together until the mixture resembles fine breadcrumbs.

Break egg into a separate bowl, add sugar and mix lightly.

Add to flour mixture and mix until pastry comes together.

Cover and refrigerate for 30 minutes.

Roll pastry to 3 mm (⅛ in) thickness. **sweet pastry tart shell**

Use pastry to line a 23 cm (9 in) buttered flan tin.

Chill for a further 30 minutes.

Preheat oven to 180ºC (350ºF/gas mark 4).

Line pastry shell with greaseproof paper.

Fill with baking beans or weights and bake for 15 minutes.

Remove paper and beans.

Bake for a further 3–4 minutes until pastry is crisp.

Tart shell is now ready to be filled.

Place the ricotta in a large bowl and mash with a fork.

Lightly whisk in zest, juice, eggs, cream, sugar, vanilla and flour.

lemon ricotta tart Pour ricotta filling into tart shell.

Bake for 35–45 minutes in a preheated oven 180°C (350°F/gas mark 4)

or until golden and firm to the touch.

Allow to cool for 10 minutes before cutting.

Serves 8

300 g (10 oz) ricotta

Grated zest of 2 lemons

3 tbsp lemon juice

3 eggs

185 ml (6 fl oz) cream

125 g (4 oz) caster sugar

1 tsp vanilla extract*

50 g (1¾ oz) plain flour

1 sweet pastry tart shell

6 eggs

Beat eggs, mascarpone, sugar, passionfruit, zest and juice together.

passionfruit tart Allow to stand for 30 minutes.

Strain to remove passionfruit pips.

Pour filling into tart shell.

Place in a preheated oven 140°C (280°F/gas mark 1).

Bake for 30 minutes, or until just set on top.

Remove and allow to cool completely before cutting.

Serves 8

125 g (8 oz) mascarpone cheese

220 g (7½ oz) caster sugar

250 ml (8 fl oz) passionfruit pulp

(approx 12–15 passionfruit)

Grated zest of 2 lemons

4 tbsp lemon juice

1 sweet pastry tart shell

Prepare frangipane by creaming butter and sugar until white.

frangipane tart Whisk in eggs and combine.

Add ground almonds and flour and stir until well combined.

Spoon frangipane mixture into tart shell.

Bake for 30 minutes, until set and golden brown.

Serve with thick cream.

Serves 8

100 g (3½ oz) soft butter

110 g (3¾ oz) caster sugar

2 eggs

100 g (3½ oz) ground almonds

20 g (¾ oz) plain flour

1 sweet pastry tart shell

barbecue wine

Right. We're out in the garden and there's a barbecue going on. The table's groaning with salads and sauces and your friends have all arrived at once. Good. Now, what are we going to drink? Beer, of course – that's an institution – a few ice-cold cans will be chilling in the fridge.

But what about wine? Surely there's room for some barbecue wines?

In my humble opinion, a wine needs to satisfy fairly strict criteria to qualify for the honour of being a great barbecue wine.

Good barbecue wine criteria

It has to be good value: if you're drinking a cheap wine, you still want to feel as though you're drinking a really good quality wine.

It also needs to be widely available at the kind of price that encourages buying more than one bottle; after all, you're probably catering for a crowd.

Barbecue wines have to be good enough to pass the distraction test. This is when a sip of a wine can get someone to say, 'Jeez, that's good. What is it?'.

Barbecue wines have to be big-flavoured, character-filled, generous, solid drinks.

These wines must taste just as good out of chunky plastic tumblers as they do out of fine crystal.

WHITE WINES

Riesling
A good, crisp, lime-juicy, young (less than a year old) riesling is sensational with shellfish – especially if there's an Asian accent to the cooking.

Sauvignon blanc
Again, pick one that's less than a year old and enjoy its pungent passionfruit and cut-grass zestiness with squid or white fish.

Verdelho
Yet again, drink it as young as you can, and get into the pineappley, tropical groove with tuna and other full-flavoured marinated fish.

Full-bodied white blends
We're talking semillon, chardonnay or white burgundy: these are great with a wide range of foods, from fish through to spicy marinated meats.

Oaked chardonnay or semillon
Choose a full, toasty, rich one and drink with chicken, chicken and, um, chicken.

RED WINES

Pinot Noir
Good pinot is good with not-too-weighty food: such as plump barbecued quail.

Grenache and grenache blends
Possibly the best barbecue wines of the lot: spicy raspberry fruit and hints of sweet game, fabulous with lots and lots of garlicky barbecued vegetables.

Shiraz
Even more possibly the best barbecue wines: go for warmer climate wines with their rich blackberry fruit and softness, great when sizzling duck, venison or sausages.

Cabernet sauvignon and cabernet blends
Sturdy wines with dark fruit and grapey tannins that match good, honest, down-to-earth steak and kebabs.

AND NOT FORGETTING

Rosé wines
My favourite barbecue wines are often rosé: they just seem to go so well with everything. They taste even better chilled and drunk out of tumblers.

Sparkling red
A barbecue just wouldn't be a barbecue if it didn't feature at least one bottle of glorious foaming purple stuff. Again, great with so many different foods, but arguably best of all with game.

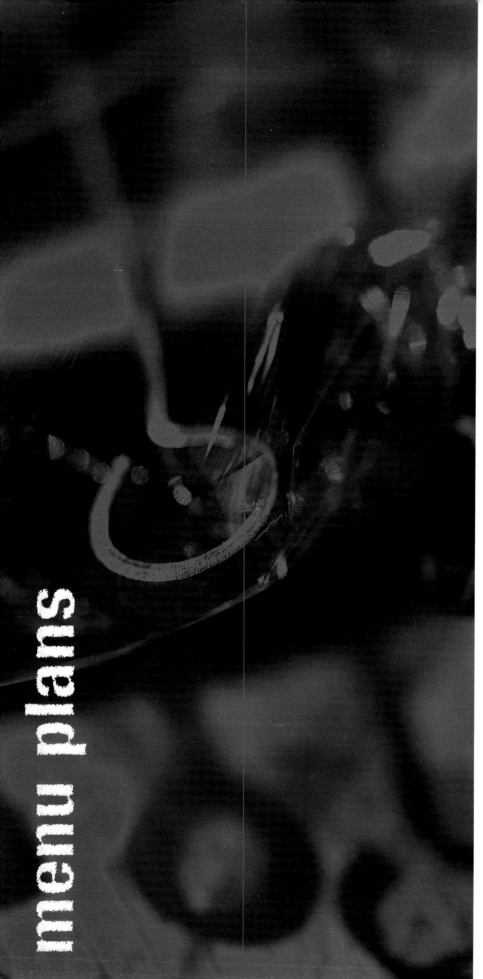

menu plans

BEACHSIDE BARBECUE

Lime and chilli chicken wings

Minty salmon kebabs

Beef burgers

Jonathan's cevapcici

Moroccan couscous salad

Lemon ricotta tart

ITALIAN INFLUENCE

Pecorino and pancetta vine leaf parcels

Balsamic chicken fillets

Rosemary lamb kebabs

Radicchio with gorgonzola

Mushroom risotto cakes

Rosewater and cardamon panne cotta
with figs

CHILDREN'S FAVOURITES

Sausages in bread

Barbecued polenta

Simple barbecued lamb

Simple pork spare ribs

Sweet paprika corn cobs

Indian bread

FINGER FOOD PARTY

Green chilli and kaffir lime
calamari skewers

Mexican spicy drumlets

Oysters two ways

Pandan chicken parcels

Beef satay kebabs

Satay pork sugar cane sticks

MAGICAL MIDDLE-EAST

Tunisian sardines

Babaganoush

Chermoula prawns with tzaziki

Lamb kofta skewers

Pomegranate and sumac glazed duck

Moroccan couscous salad

Frangipane tart

VEGETARIAN SPECIAL

Polenta corn cakes

Caramelised onion
and chickpea burgers

Tofu spicy kebabs

Vegetable kebabs

Tomatoes with basil butter

Plum clafouti

INDIAN

Indian bread

Chicken tandoori

Kashmiri quail

Indian tikka lamb

CELEBRATION BBQ

Crayfish with roasted
red pepper butter

Whole smoky salmon

Moroccan barbecued turkey

Watercress tabouleh

Potato salad

Rosé poached berries with shortbread

ASIAN AROMAS

Scallops with wasabi and ginger butter

Pandan chicken parcels

Oriental chicken

Korean fiery beef

Soy and ginger salmon

Simple bok choy salad

Asian coleslaw

JAPANESE

Tuna teriyaki skewers

Shoyu beef

Tea-scented sticky duck

Asian noodle salad

BBQ BONANZA

Sizzlin' garlic prawns

Barbecued whole fish

Whole barbecued chicken

The perfect steak

Jonathan's cevapcici

BBQ sauce

Green salad

Garlic mushrooms

Potato wedges

Pavlova with berries

[glossary]

Arborio rice
Short grain rice from northern Italy used for making risotto.

Banana leaves
Available from Asian grocers, these large green leaves can be used to wrap food during cooking. They impart little flavour, but make a big impression at the table. Kitchen foil can be used instead.

Bean paste
Every Asian country has its own version of bean paste, Japanese miso being the most widely known. All can be substituted for one another as they all have an intense, salty flavour. Chinese bean paste is often mixed with chillies.

Black beans
Fermented salted black beans require soaking in water for at least 10 minutes before being rinsed, drained and chopped. Available in cans from large supermarkets or Asian shops.

Black pepper
All pepper is freshly ground black pepper, unless otherwise stated.

Bok choy
Small bundles of Oriental leafy green cabbages.

Bulgar wheat
Cracked wheat grain. Soak for 30 minutes in cold water to soften before use.

Chermoula
Middle-Eastern spice blend.

Chilli jam
A blend of chillies, fried shallots, sugar and other flavourings with a jam-like consistency.

Chilli paste
A fiery chilli mixture also called *sambal oelek*. Adjust amounts to suit your taste.

Coconut milk/cream
Made from grated coconut that is soaked in hot water. Coconut milk is lighter than coconut cream, which is the thickest part, skimmed off the surface of the milk.

Cornichons
Pickled baby cucumbers; also called gherkins.

Couscous
This staple of North African cooking comes in different grades. 'Instant' couscous requires soaking in boiling water. Couscous is a type of semolina.

Daikon radish
Large white radish, most commonly used in Japanese cuisine.

Dukkah
Egyptian spice mix consisting of ground spices, nuts and sesame seeds.

Five-spice powder
A Chinese blend usually containing cloves, anise, cinnamon, pepper and fennel.

Gelatine
Substance derived from animal bones and used to set desserts and puddings. Sheet gelatine is considered better than powdered gelatine.

Grated ginger
Approx 5 cm (2 in) of fresh root ginger will produce 1 tsp of grated ginger. Ginger graters (small white ceramic graters) are available from Asian grocers.

Harissa
Tunisian chilli paste with a smoky flavour.

Herbs
All herbs are fresh unless otherwise stated.

Indonesian soy sauce
Thick and sweet, Indonesian soy sauce is also known as *kecap manis*. It can be substituted by a combination of soy sauce and sugar, but this sauce is available at Asian grocers.

Kaffir lime leaves
Search out fresh leaves from Asian grocers. Each leaf consists of two oval sections with a pungent citrus flavour. Mostly used whole in broths for flavour, or shredded finely for salads and marinades. If you cannot get Kaffir lime leaves, use strips of lime zest instead.

Lemongrass
Long, tough stems with a fibrous quality and a light lemony flavour. Use to add a lemon taste to food or as 'natural' skewers.

Mascarpone
Fresh Italian cheese with a rich sour cream flavour. Usually used in desserts.

Mirin
Sweetened Japanese sake used for cooking.

Olive oil
Extra virgin olive oil has a finer flavour than olive oil, but use one that suits your tastes and budget.

Palm sugar
Sugar made from the sap of palm trees set into thick dense cakes. Best shaved with a sharp knife when needed. Usually dissolved in an acidic liquid such as lemon juice or fish sauce. Use soft brown sugar or light muscovado as an alternative.

Pancetta
Smoked Italian bacon.

Pandan leaves
Long, flat emerald green leaves with a delicate scent. Used to wrap food during cooking or to add flavour to rice dishes. Use banana leaves or kitchen foil as an alternative when making parcels.

Parmesan cheese
True Parmigiano Reggiano comes only from Italy. Be sure you are buying Parmigiano (or *grana padano*), rather than imitation Parmesan.

Pomegranate syrup
Thick bittersweet fruit syrup available from Middle-Eastern grocery stores.

Prosciutto
Also known as Parma ham, this salted, air-dried ham adds a salty, bacon flavour to dishes.

Red chilli
Small red chillies (not bird's eye) are used unless otherwise stated. Take care removing seeds and membranes as these contain the capsaicin (source of the heat).

Rice flour/ground rice
Finely ground rice used to make shortbread and other biscuits.

Rice vinegar
Rice vinegar is a product of Japan. Make sure you purchase pure rice vinegar, not flavoured vinegar sold as 'sushi vinegar'.

Rice wine
Chinese rice wine has a delicate amber colour and gentle fragrance. Can substitute dry sherry at a pinch.

Rosewater
Rose-scented liquid from the Middle-East. Available at delicatessens and large supermarkets.

Saffron
Saffron is one of the world's most expensive spices, with each thread coming from the centre of the crocus flower. Luckily only a few threads are needed to enjoy saffron's aroma and flavour.

Salt
Use sea salt for preference, as it has a finer mineral flavour than common table salt. Some recipes call for sea salt flakes.

Sesame oil
A rich aromatic oil made from roasted sesame seeds. Only a small amount is needed to add flavour to dishes.

Shallots
Small brown or red onion-like vegetables. Red shallots are used extensively in Asian cuisines, and have a flavour between garlic and onion.

Shiitake mushrooms
Asian mushrooms with a firm texture and meaty mushroom flavour. Available in supermarkets.

Shoyu
Japanese soy sauce.

Sichuan pepper
Also known as Szechwan or Szechuan pepper. These small red berries, while not actually members of the pepper family, have a peppery taste. Best toasted before use.

Sugar cane
Sometimes available fresh; if not, they are available canned from Asian grocers. Soak well in cold water before use to remove 'tinned' flavour.

Sumac
Ground red berries with a sweet and sour flavour. Available from Middle-Eastern grocery stores

Tahini
Paste made from sesame seeds. Look in Middle-Eastern grocery stores or the health food section of the supermarket.

Tamari
Japanese wheat-free soy sauce.

Tamarind water
Tamarind pulp is sold in clear plastic tubs. Soak 30 g (1 oz) of the sour tamarind pulp in 125 ml (4 fl oz) of boiling water. Strain, discard the pulp, allow to cool then use remaining water.

Thai basil
Fragrant leafy herb with strong spicy flavour. It has purple stems and serrated leaves.

Thai fish sauce
A tangy thin sauce made from salted fish and essential in many Asian cuisines. Wonderful for adding a salty flavour burst to food.

Tofu
Also called bean curd. Firm varieties are best suited to barbecuing. Needs long marinating to absorb flavours.

Vanilla extract
As the name suggests, this is a pure extraction of crushed vanilla pods producing a thick, aromatic liquid. Use it wherever vanilla is called for. Vanilla essence is a poor substitute.

Vine leaves
If using fresh vine leaves, cook in boiling water until tender. If using preserved vine leaves, rinse well under cold water. Leaves are edible.

Wasabi
Fiery lime-green paste used extensively in Japanese cuisine. Tastes like horseradish.

Water chestnuts
Aquatic vegetable that retains its crunchy texture when cooked. Occasionally available fresh in Asian greengrocers but most usually canned.

[**index**]

Left to right: Adrian Lander, Max Allen, Michele Curtis, Allan Campion and Ian Scott.

Food writers Allan Campion and Michele Curtis, and graphic designer Ian Scott have built an enviable reputation for books that combine inspirational food content with innovative design.

Adrian Lander trained as a chef in England, then discovered a passion for photography while working in Austria. Adrian's work has featured in numerous magazines and books, including *Chalk and Cheese,* Max Allen's *Red and White* and *Banc* by Stan Sarris and Liam Tomlin.

Max Allen is one of Australia's favourite wine writers. When he's not scribbling a weekly column in *The Australian Magazine* or editing the *Wine Planet* web site, Max can usually be found slaving over a sizzling grill, glass of rosé in one hand, pair of tongs in the other.

Conversion chart

Measurements in recipes are meant as a guide only. The conversions are approximate, a teaspoon or two difference in a recipe will rarely ruin it. Always prepare food to your own tastes.

Celsius	Fahrenheit	Millilitres	Fluid Ounces	Grams	Ounces
120°	245°	5 ml	1 tsp	5 g	1 tsp
140°	280°	10 ml	2 tsp 1 dessertspoon	10 g	2 tsp
150°	300°	15 ml	½ fl oz 1 tablespoon	15 g	½ oz
160°	320°	20 ml	⅔ fl oz	20 g	⅔ oz
170°	340°	30 ml	1 fl oz	30 g	1 oz
180°	350°	40 ml	1⅓ fl oz	40 g	1⅓ oz
190°	375°	50 ml	1⅔ fl oz	50 g	1⅔ oz
200°	390°	60 ml	2 fl oz	60 g	2 oz
210°	410°	75 ml	2½ fl oz	75 g	2½ oz
220°	425°	80 ml	2⅔ fl oz	80 g	2⅔ oz
230°	450°	100 ml	3½ fl oz	100 g	3½ oz
		125 ml	4 fl oz	125 g	4 oz
		150 ml	5 fl oz	150 g	5 oz
		200 ml	7 fl oz	200 g	7 oz
		250 ml	8 fl oz	250 g	8 oz (½ lb)
		300 ml	10 fl oz (½ pt)	300 g	10 oz
		400 ml	13 fl oz	400 g	13 oz
		500 ml	16 fl oz	500 g (½ kg)	16 oz (1 lb)